Praise for *Lessons from Emily*

Emily Jones was a rare spirit. In love with the world and all its possibilities. Eager to show others the wonder she felt. She was a teacher of the highest order. Her kindness mended people who knew her. I did not know her like a sister or a daughter, but I am so lucky to have met her. Her sense of hope was as real as the ocean or the sky. Emily was and is an angel. Thanks to both her and her family for the time I spent with them.

—Dave Matthews, front man, guitarist,
singer-songwriter, Dave Matthews Band

One cannot help but be spiritually affected by the amazing story of Emily Jones, an angel sent to Earth for the express purpose of teaching us lessons on not only how to live but how to die, as well. This young girl's story of faith will strengthen your own.

—Lynn Coffey, author of *Backroads*,
a four-book series about
Virginia's disappearing Appalachian culture

Lessons from Emily is the story of what is arguably the most heart-wrenching of all human events: the death of one's beloved child. With great sensitivity, Caroline Jones has gifted us with the writing of her family's faith-filled journey as their young daughter, Emily, bravely battles an unusually cruel cancer. Emily's lessons are many. Among them, she teaches the reader to live life as fully as possible and to believe in the ultimate goodness of God's love for His people. All who read this book will be enriched in their faith.

—Terry Jones-Brady, author of
*A Mosaic Heart: Reshaping the Shards
of a Shattered Life*

Emily Caroline Jones is a forever inspiration . . . her ministry began with her very existence and the relationships she formed with her smile, her heart, and her wit. It continues through her eternal watch and, now, her mother's lovingly penned words. As Emily's first dance teacher, I bear witness to the fact that the love and faith she absorbed from her family and her God provided her with the wind beneath her wings to enjoy her dreams of dancing and teaching . . . we danced together, and I continue to learn and spread her lessons in my second career as an elementary school teacher. So many parallels in our lives, Emily's and mine, and now I feel both compelled and honoured to continue her legacy of education, for I have been given the gift of time on earth [with which] to carry our dreams forward.

—Abi Henneberry, teacher and dancer

I vividly remember the day, two decades ago, when I met the little girl named Emily Jones, who boldly and beautifully wrote her personal story for the magazine where I'd recently been hired as an editor. I had no idea at the time that her mother is also a gifted scribe, who has revisited powerful emotions to share Emily's sweet yet fierce determination in faith through physical challenges. The day I visited thirteen-year-old Emily, her big smile and bright eyes flashed fearlessly as she announced, very proudly, that she was the only child ever to contract the adults-only disease I still don't quite know how to properly pronounce.

In the same way that Emily was able to shine light on a seemingly dark situation, Caroline Jones writes of her daughter's hospital stays and health struggles in a way that wraps it in loveliness, never coming off as clinical or even depressing. Yes, I dropped a few tears as I read, but only because I felt upliftment or compassion, not despair. I can almost see Emily now, bearing a supergirl-style badge of bravery on her chest, a C that stands not for cancer but Courage. *Lessons from Emily* isn't a tale of death—it's a wonderful testament to life everlasting.

—Kelly Anne White, author of the upcoming
Jesus Groupie (releasing October 2014)

Lessons
from
Emily

A Story of Faith,
Courage, and Love

Caroline Carter Jones

To God be the glory!
Caroline Carter Jones

Quarter Books

Cover design by Jane Hagaman
Interior design by Jane Hagaman

The cover image is a portion of a quilt, "Pandora's Box," created by
Emily Jones in 1995.

Unless otherwise noted, scripture taken from the *Holy Bible,
New International Version*®. Copyright © 1973, 1978, 1984
by International Bible Society. Used by permission of Zondervan.
All rights reserved.

LORD OF THE DANCE
by Sydney Carter
© 1963 Stainer & Bell, Ltd. (Admin. Hope Publishing Company,
Carol Stream, IL 60188). All rights reserved. Used by permission.

Book production by:
Quartet Books
Charlottesville, VA
www.quartetbooks.com

If you are unable to order this book from your local bookseller,
you may order directly from the author at P. O. Box 384,
Fishersville, VA 22939 or at her website: www.lessonsfromemily.com.

Library of Congress Control Number: 2014936398

ISBN 978-0-9914692-0-8

10 9 8 7 6 5 4 3 2 1

Printed on acid-free paper in the United States

For my grandchildren,
who would have delighted in their Auntie Emily,
just as she would have delighted in them.

Contents

Preface

In 1983, my family and I moved out of our starter home into a bigger one. The new place—the Alleghany house, as we called it—was brick, had a front porch, a big yard, and enough bedrooms so that no one had to double up for sleeping. The front door opened into a huge living room that had a fireplace and built-in book-shelves on the far end. The living room opened into a big dining room with a built-in corner cupboard and room for two other antique corner cupboards plus my grandmother's dining room table and chairs, my mom's sideboard, and a library table made by my grandfather.

Behind the dining room was a small porch that had been enclosed to make a family room. The kitchen was long and narrow with outdated appliances. In fact, the oven door didn't close all the way, but we were told it still worked "just fine." The most amazing first-floor feature was the tiny door that led to the basement. This "fairy" door was only about four feet high and two feet wide. An average person had to squeeze through it to get to the basement steps. The only other way to the basement was to go outside and enter through the garage.

The second floor had three bedrooms, a small bath, and a stor-age room. The master bedroom was upstairs. It had 1950s-vintage wallpaper—big feathers with silver flowers—and no heat, since the only duct was sealed with concrete and bricks when the porch was converted into a family room. The two larger bedrooms had slanted, roof-line ceilings. The smallest upstairs bedroom was sandwiched between the master bedroom and bath. It had a little dormer window overlooking the backyard and cemetery beyond.

In spite of its many quirks, I had a good feeling about the house. It seemed happy and inviting. It even came with a cat! Actually, the previous owners took their cat with them, but he ran away almost immediately and after about a week returned to "his" home on Alleghany Avenue. By mutual agreement, we let him stay. Toughie lived with us until our younger daughter Emily's allergies prompted his permanent eviction to a friend's farm.

As much as I loved the house, my husband saw a money pit. I admit that many improvements were needed, especially since my mom would live with us. She had been disabled since she contracted polio while serving as an Army nurse in North Africa and Italy during World War II, and Jerry and I were pleased to have enough room for her to join us.

First on the renovation list was the installation of a standard door to replace the "fairy" door. Next, we remodeled the kitchen and converted two rooms on the main floor into a large bath with a closet for the washer and dryer (which had been in the basement) and a comfortable bedroom for my mom. The whole house was rewired, and a breaker box was added to replace the existing fuse box. We also added a concrete porch across much of the back of the house and steps and a ramp leading to the driveway to make it handicapped accessible.

Several months after the major renovations were finished, Jerry decided that the asbestos that lined the heating ducts should be removed. This undertaking was expensive and a little spooky. He contracted a company that specialized in asbestos removal to do the work. Plastic sheeting was used to create a protected entrance into the basement through the garage. The workmen wore special white bodysuits and air-filter masks; they had to shower before leaving the worksite. Huge, flexible vacuum hoses stretched from their van into our basement. Air quality tests were conducted at regular intervals throughout the removal process and for several weeks afterward.

For more than a week, our house bore a resemblance to the scene in the movie *ET* when ET was quarantined as an alien specimen while the human scientists examined him.

Because I had heard that asbestos wasn't dangerous unless it was disturbed, I wasn't convinced that we needed to go to the time and expense of having it removed. Jerry, however, was insistent. A little more than twelve years later he told me why.

You see, "thoughts" sometimes come to my husband. For example, in early spring 2001, he had an overwhelming feeling that something terrible was going to happen and that it would involve airplanes. Much blood would be spilled. The feeling was so strong that he determined we should not follow through on plans to travel abroad later in the year. He silently harbored the disturbing fear that something would happen to our twenty-three-year-old daughter, who that summer traveled to Europe as part of a church mission team.

I knew nothing of his concerns until the afternoon of September 11, 2001—the afternoon of the terrorist attacks that changed America forever. We were leaving a cemetery following the funeral of a dear friend. As we walked toward our car, Jerry turned to me and said, "I thought we had gotten through the summer without anything happening." Baffled, I asked him what he meant. He explained about the feeling of extreme dread that he had experienced months earlier, about his fear for Ann and his prayers that covered her while she was away. I then understood why he had not pursued our trip to Europe. It was eerie and frightening to realize just how accurate his premonition had been.

Jerry also had a premonition shortly after moving into our Alleghany house. This premonition involved our children—one of the girls would have cancer while living there. Removing the asbestos was Jerry's plan to eliminate the possibility. Had I known about it, we would never have spent one night in that house. Jerry would tell me years later that he did not believe the cancer was *because of the house*—just while we were *in the house*. I found little consolation in that distinction.

By the time Emily was four, those of us who knew and loved her—that is, her parents, sister, grandparents, aunts, uncles, cousins, and a host of friends—knew two great truths about her: She would dance, and she would follow the beat of a different drummer. Dance came easily to Emily. Following the beat of a different drummer challenged the very depths of her spirit, causing her to walk through the fiery furnace. She emerged as gold, a victor in an unspeakable battle. Perhaps as a hint of what was to come, when she was just six or seven years old she drew a picture of a trumpet. On it she printed: "I will be a trumpter [sic] for God." She had no idea how that bold statement would play out in her life.

I once heard that the birth and death dates on a tombstone are of little value; it is what a person does between those dates that matters. The dates on Emily's tombstone span just fourteen years, but she made every one count. One-seventh of her life was spent battling cancer. In spite of the ugliness of her illness, she developed an unshakable faith. She became an extraordinary witness in trusting God, even unto death. Her story is powerful. It is absolutely true.

Emily Caroline Jones had one career goal—to be a teacher. Though she never had a chance to take courses in education, she mastered the art of teaching. She taught us how to live—and how to die. The lessons in this book are written not only to honor her memory but also to glorify God. I know she would want it that way.

Praise the Lord!

Caroline Carter Jones
August 2014

Acknowledgments

I began writing Emily's story several months after she passed away. It sat unfinished for many years until I shared it with my dear friend and mentor, Nancy Ellen Artis, who believed that Emily's story should be told and that I was the one to do it. I am deeply grateful for her faith in me. It is she who made this book possible.

I wish to thank the kind ladies in the Medical Records Department of the University of Virginia Hospital. They graciously copied approximately one thousand pages of Emily's medical records and patiently sat with me for hours while I reviewed the material.

A sincere, heartfelt thank you goes to Ann Simmons, who was the first official reader of the manuscript. Her thoughts and memories were especially helpful.

Deep gratitude is extended to David Reed and Barbara Sawyer, whose spiritual insights and comments gave me faith to persevere.

Emily Stumb was invaluable in improving the quality of some of the pictures used in this book.

My sister, Ann Carter, and a friend, Carolynn Van Dyke, read the manuscript with their hearts as well as their minds, and their suggestions lifted the book to a higher plane.

Kelly Anne White, author and former editor of *Girls' Life* magazine, gave freely of her time, talents, and encouragement in the final writing stages of the book. Her thoughts and suggestions were invaluable.

My heart overflows with thanksgiving for my daughter, Ann, and my son-in-law, Davison Long. Words cannot describe the love I have for them and their children, in whom I so often see glimmers of my Emily.

Finally, I wish to acknowledge my husband, whose love and support were paramount to the completion of this book. I am thankful beyond measure that he always listens to the "still, small voice" within him. His wisdom, heart, and soul are embedded in every page of this book.

Part 1

1993–1994

Even though I walk

through the valley of the

   shadow of death,

I will fear no evil,

for you are with me;

your rod and your staff,

they comfort me.

—Psalm 23:4

Chapter 1

Point those toes!

—note written by Emily
on a homeroom card,
September 1993

"Mom! Mom!"

Emily's urgent call jarred me awake. Grabbing my glasses, I quickly walked the few steps from my bedroom into Emily's tiny one. In the soft glow of her nightlight I could see my twelve-year-old daughter propped on one arm as she leaned over the trash can.

Since moving into the Alleghany Avenue house ten years earlier, Emily had never felt comfortable sleeping without some sort of light. Often she called to her dad and me that she heard voices at her second floor window. "Aliens," she called them, alluding to the people who were buried in the beautiful old cemetery just behind our gray-brick, 1920s-vintage house.

"Don't worry, Emily," her daddy had assured her. "If they're aliens, they're friendly. Now go to sleep." Tonight, though, she did not seem to be concerned with the voices as she rubbed her stomach with her free hand.

"I'm going to throw up," she said. "Stay with me."

I pushed aside several of her beloved stuffed animals as she drew her feet close under her chin. Sitting with her on her white rattan daybed, I rested my hand on her leg and looked at her face; she seemed comforted now by the presence of her mother.

Over the years, I had sat with Emily many times during late-night battles with asthma, counting her respirations while debating whether to call the doctor. More than once my husband and I had packed her into the car for dashes to the emergency room for breathing treatments. Following the advice of her allergist, however, years earlier we had found a new home for our beloved family cat and had removed the wall-to-wall carpet. After shoveling up bags of rotted carpet padding, beautiful hardwood floors were revealed and area rugs made it much easier to control dust and other allergens. For several years now, Emily's asthma had been well managed and had not caused significant problems except during high pollen seasons. Because I could hear no wheezing, I knew the nausea was not asthma-related.

"Here it comes, Mom."

And so it did. Emily threw up two or three times into the plastic liner of her trash can, after which she laid her head on the pillow and sleepily stated that she felt much better. After waiting for several more minutes to see if she were truly better, I marveled that this child could at one minute experience racking nausea and the next appear quite well. "Isn't that just like Emily?" I thought. "Nothing bothers her for long."

In the quiet of that night, I looked around her crowded little room and smiled as I saw Emily's vibrant personality everywhere— from the dolls that sat neatly in their assigned seats on the shelf, hugging each other contentedly, to the many posters of dancers that adorned her walls. "Daddy, let me put these up, p-l-e-a-s-e," she had successfully begged.

Her wish granted, a favorite ballerina poster was soon taped on her closet door, visible even at this late hour in the soft glow of the nightlight. Beneath the picture were these words:

If you can imagine it, you can achieve it.
If you can dream it, you can become it.

—*William Arthur Ward*

"Sweet Emily," I thought to myself. "You're some kid."

Satisfied that she was not going to vomit again, I stood to leave her room. She smiled at me and held her arms outstretched, waiting for the hug she knew I could not resist. As I bent down, Emily wrapped her arms tightly around my neck and whispered, "I love you!" in my ear. I returned the words before letting go. Turning to leave her room, I paused at the door. From there we blew kisses to one another, each locking the received blessing in her own heart, a loving gesture we had repeated countless nights before. I padded softly back to my own bed. I glanced at the clock before removing my glasses. It was one thirty Friday morning, November 27, 1993.

"Is Emily okay?" my groggy but concerned husband whispered, remembering that Emily had been unable to eat much of her Thanksgiving dinner the day before.

"Yes," I replied. "She threw up several times but seems fine now. Maybe she has a virus. Anyway, she went right back to sleep. It must not be anything." As I drifted back into my own deep sleep, I did not know, nor could I have imagined, that this simple episode of nausea opened the final chapter of Emily's life.

It seemed we had waited forever for this moment: Emily was ready to go *en pointe*—known to the layperson as toe dancing. As she was fitted for her first pair of steel-toed pointe shoes, I was reminded of a time six years earlier when Emily, not yet in kindergarten, was fitted for her first pair of ballet slippers. Her tiny but wide feet belied the power of her will to dance.

At the age of five, Emily barely weighed thirty-five pounds. Her petite hands and feet were complemented by enormous, sparkling green eyes. Her big smile revealed a chipped front tooth, knocked out one summer evening as she looped around the iron railing of our gray painted–brick front steps. Her nose and cheeks were peppered with big freckles. Her auburn brown hair was thick, straight, and long. Emily often wore it pulled back, the swing in her walk mirrored by the swing in her beribboned ponytail.

Undaunted by her size or her asthma, Emily begged me to find a place where she could learn to dance. Due to conflicts with my teaching schedule, the closest studio with evening and Saturday classes for five-year-olds was Abi's *Pas de Chat* in Harrisonburg, a city about thirty-five miles north of our home in Staunton, Virginia.

As a four-year-old, Emily had joined her six-and-a-half-year-old sister, Ann, in gymnastics lessons. Emily's asthma flared frequently, however, and she missed as many classes as she attended. Recognizing that her asthma might again prevent Emily from becoming truly invested, I reluctantly paid the fee for her first semester in a beginner's level dance class. Before long, Ann dropped gymnastics and picked up dancing, too. Dance didn't turn out to be Ann's thing, so she stuck with it for only a couple of years.

Emily, however, began to live her dream. Early on she bonded with Abi Henneberry, a young, energetic, and dedicated dance teacher. Week after week we made the seventy-mile round trip to Harrisonburg. At recital time, we made two or three trips per week. Unlike her working mother, Emily never tired of the time or travel commitment. She just wanted to dance. Even with my gentle nudging, she refused to consider leaving Abi's program to enter dance classes nearer home. Not until Abi married and moved away did Emily consent to enrolling in a local program.

As Emily sat on the floor, patiently trying on pair after pair of pointe shoes, I recognized that her spirit and determination were solidly intact. Following Abi's marriage and move, Emily soon lobbied to join classes at the local Staunton Academy of Ballet (SAB). While I missed Abi and the group of mothers whom I had joined weekly for more than four years, I was thrilled with the convenience of a three-block drive to dance lessons.

Although Emily was now eleven, freckles continued to accentuate her nose and cheeks, and her hair was still long and straight. Her large green eyes retained their clear, penetrating quality. Her hands, no longer petite, were marked by long and elegant fingers. Her nails were manicured and often sported bright and shocking preadolescent colors. Her dancer's neck and straight body lines were characteristic of the dancer she aspired to be.

How Emily adored her lovely pink pointe shoes! She could not resist the urge to practice the *plié*, *Battement tendu*, and *pirouette* while gripping the mantelpiece in the den for balance. Up and down she went, over and over again, determined to master this or that move. Before long, she was walking in her toe shoes from the den to the bathroom and back. She spent hours in front of a semi-long mirror, arms arched over her head, hands in the "teacup" position. Whatever she lacked in skill, she made up for in dogged determination. This child would dance.

Over the years, along with outgrown dance shoes, Emily's closet filled with recital costumes, each one a treasure and having a story all its own. While Abi's recitals were theme-based, at SAB Emily had the chance to dance in full-length ballets, including *Swan Lake, Giselle*, and *The Nutcracker*. Her costumes are all packed away now, some stained from years of dress-up play, some torn, some never worn after a performance, but each one a silent reminder of one little girl's passion to dance and create.

In May 1993, tryouts were held for the local production of *The Nutcracker,* which would be performed the second weekend of December. Emily had danced in earlier productions, but this year her entire dance class would perform two numbers *en pointe*, as well as participate in the opening scene, known as "The Party."

That fall, excitement ran high and practices ran long, but Emily never complained.

In elementary school, Emily sometimes had to attend "Homework Club" before the start of the school day, not because she was a poor student but because she often liked to dilly-dally at night. She loved television and every opportunity to play. Her dad and I, even though we were both in public education, felt that our girls were responsible for their own homework. That is not to say we were not available to help when needed—we were—but we wanted them to accept ownership of their roles as students. As a seventh grader, Emily was able to keep up with her assignments while spending many long nights in rehearsal.

Emily's post-Thanksgiving nausea that November was of little concern to me at the time. She had seemed fine the following day. On Monday, Emily returned to school and to serious rehearsals lasting long hours. All seemed well. Over the next two weeks, she vomited once or twice more—always in the middle of the night. It was easy to ignore these episodes, since she was fine during the day. She never complained of feeling ill.

When Emily vomited again the night before her dress rehearsal, I thought she might have an unusual case of nerves. Maybe she was feeling the pinch of erratic practice times, schoolwork that needed to be done, excitement, and just plain exhaustion. Often the rehearsals would last until ten at night or later. To give her a chance to rest before the big dance weekend, I allowed her to stay home from school on the Friday of the dress rehearsal. After all, counting the dress rehearsal, she would give three performances in three days.

Videotaping was permitted only at the dress rehearsal. We did not own a camcorder, but I borrowed one from the elementary school where I was a teacher. That Friday night I sat in the darkened auditorium among dozens of other proud parents, cameras poised to capture every move made by their own rising stars.

As the last notes of the overture concluded, the curtain opened on "The Party." My heart raced with anticipation as the first dancers came on stage. Suddenly there she was—my Emily—her hair bouncing and lively in the old-fashioned ringlets created by wrapping section after section of hair in torn sheets. She was really beautiful—graceful and elegant in her green satin dress with the long sash and frilly bloomers. "Mine's the prettiest dress, Mom. Everyone says so," Emily had boasted to me.

"Would you look at that," I thought as my pounding heart swelled with pride. I could barely resist the urge to lower my camera and crow out loud. But, of course, I just kept taping. I'm positive that parents all around me were likewise silently applauding their own prima ballerinas. Without a doubt, I was in great company that night. And though my arm grew tired and my fingers numb, I zoomed the lens in and out, all the time focused on my sweet baby as she glided across the stage on her toes, her face radiant with the joy of dancing.

With the dress rehearsal behind her, Emily's "real" *Nutcracker* performances followed on Saturday night and Sunday afternoon. She was exuberant, knowing that nearly an entire row of the auditorium would be occupied by her admirers. Family members, including grandparents, made up most of the row. A dear college friend also came with her son, Ryan. He was enthralled by Emily and the whole production. In fact, with a ten-year-old's admiration and sincerity, he promised that he would never see another production of *The Nutcracker.* I won't hold Ryan to that promise, but I love the sweetness that was behind it.

We left the auditorium in a rush that afternoon after Emily's final performance because she said that she didn't feel well. She clutched the traditional bouquet of flowers and a just-purchased miniature wooden nutcracker. Were her thoughts on future performances when her skill level would open the door to more coveted solo roles? Or were they on the pain that was brewing in her belly? I will never know. What I do know is that on that Sunday afternoon in early December 1993, Emily danced her final performance of *The Nutcracker*.

With the dance rehearsals and two public performances over, we began the business of preparing for Christmas. It would be fair to say that, next to dance, Emily's biggest love was decorating. Every holiday—indeed, every occasion—presented an opportunity to adorn the living and dining rooms with streamers, balloons, banners, or anything else that remotely fit the occasion. Faithfully every year at Thanksgiving, she and Ann lobbied to bring the Christmas decorations out of storage. Putting off this time-consuming and dusty task was easy as long as Emily was involved with dancing. Now that we could stall no longer, the hanging of the greens began in earnest. Soon our house was in full holiday regalia.

Assuming its place of honor, the 1950s nativity was carefully positioned on the living room mantelpiece. This beloved cardboard centerpiece passed down to me when my mother, whom we called Bubbles, came to live with us several years after my father's death. For at least forty Christmases it had been the focal point of our holiday decorating, with three generations of believers arranging and rearranging the principal characters. Even though some of the paint had worn off Mary and Joseph and the three Wise Men, all of the pieces were present and accounted for. Even the angel, who year after year perched precariously on the steeply sloped and almost strawless roof, had not a single chip or crack in her golden wings.

I don't know if it is typical of most children, but Emily was very drawn to the nativity. This fact was poignantly demonstrated one morning a few days before Christmas when she slipped downstairs before anyone else was awake and arranged some of her favorite dolls around a pretend manger. Raggedy Ann and Andy were Mary and Joseph. Several Cabbage Patch dolls and her Precious Moments Indian Princess were the Wise Men. Her first doll, a floppy, wild-haired baby with eyes that opened and closed, was the baby Jesus. All of us were humbled by her simple act of faith. Trite though the expression is, Emily knew the "reason for the season."

As much as Emily was captivated by the Christmas story, she also dearly loved getting—and giving—presents. Weeks before the dolls' nativity appeared, I had ordered a china crèche for her. It was to be one of Santa's special surprises. How Emily's eyes sparkled as she tore through the wrapping paper to find a box containing her very own moss-covered wooden stable with beautifully painted figurines. She wasted little time clearing the living room coffee table and arranging the assortment of characters and animals.

Often we would wake up to find one new arrangement, then another. At the close of the holiday season, she refused to store the treasured set back in the box. Instead, she cleared the bottom shelf of a bookcase in her bedroom, and there she set up the stable and all of its figures. It remained there for the rest of her life.

Decorating our house for Christmas today lacks much of the fanfare of those years, but no matter what, the kitchen window is always adorned with a small tree whose branches are filled with angel ornaments that were given to Emily during the two years that she was sick. Sometimes we put up a larger tree in the living room or sunroom. The old cardboard crèche is displayed, though not always on the mantel. And, of course, Emily's china crèche is arranged on the coffee table or washstand, just as she would want it.

Even the holiday mood could not erase a persistent uneasy feeling I had as Emily's bouts of vomiting continued. Not only were they more frequent, they were occurring in the early evening hours and continuing into the late night. She had also begun to crave ice. Hour after hour she would lie on the couch, chewing a succession of cubes while watching television. I remember being annoyed by the constant crunching.

By the time school was out for the Christmas holiday, Emily was too ill to enjoy herself. Only on Christmas morning did she seem even remotely like herself, hopping out of bed first to awaken the rest of the household and gather us in the living room to find Santa's surprises and open gifts. For that one morning, we sat sleepy-eyed, happy, and content as we opened packages. Finally, things were normal. But by supper, she was again vomiting. The time had come to call the doctor.

Blood work done at Emily's first visit to the pediatrician on December 27 revealed that she was anemic. Iron supplements were prescribed. The doctor examined her belly but found nothing unusual. To be certain he was not missing something, an upper GI was ordered for the next morning at our local hospital. The results were unremarkable. In addition to the iron supplements, Maalox was prescribed to help control overproduction of stomach acid. Even though Emily had a low-grade fever, her doctor seemed to think she would feel better within a few days.

Therefore do not worry about tomorrow,

for tomorrow will worry about itself.

Each day has enough trouble of its own.

–Matthew 6:34

As she sat on the examination table, pain free at the moment and in no apparent discomfort, I remember thinking that her longtime pediatrician might consider me an overanxious mother who sought medical attention when none was needed. That day, we left the doctor's office hoping that the worst was over. The entry in

Emily's journal for December 28–30 was, however, a more accurate record of the storm that was brewing. She wrote, "I'm fine for now."

As the New Year drew closer, Emily's condition quickly worsened. Her vomiting intensified to a frightening level. She had almost no appetite. She forced herself to eat small amounts of food, but whatever she ate remained in her stomach only minutes before being projected out. I was terrified, but I could not let it show.

Like all other holidays, New Year's Eve was vigorously celebrated in our household. Typically, we stayed home, choosing to join millions of other TV onlookers as the famous "Big Apple" crystal ball dropped into the new year. Three generations—Bubbles, Jerry and I, and Ann and Emily—would tap together wine glasses filled with sparkling grape juice to make traditional toasts. But the dawning of 1994 brought little excitement to our house. There were no toasts, no wishes extended for a bright and happy future. Instead we offered silent prayers for an end to Emily's racking nausea.

Emily was a goal setter. Determined to follow her regular routine, she returned to school at the end of the Christmas break. Every day she came home sick.

"Mom, I can't understand it," she said to me one afternoon in the office of the school where I worked. "My jeans are loose in the waist when I get up in the morning, but they're too tight to keep buttoned by the time I get home."

She looked drained and weary. Her face was pale and she was losing weight. All the while, the vomiting continued to intensify.

I didn't recall it at the time, but Emily's comment about her expandable waistline had an uncanny parallel to something a friend had told me seventeen years earlier. It was 1975, and I had just started my first teaching job in a newly opened elementary school in Charles County, Maryland. Jerry had been hired as a visiting teacher in Virginia's Augusta County school system. Some might call it coincidence, but I prefer to believe it was the mysterious hand of God that led us to begin our professional careers in different states. We had completed our master's degrees—Jerry in counseling and me in special education. We knew that finding jobs in our fields would be difficult, but, perhaps naively, we had assumed we would be together.

Few people know this about me, but from childhood into adulthood, I was plagued by a fear of abandonment. Until I was maybe nine or ten, the local dairy delivered milk twice weekly to customers. Before going to bed around eleven, my parents would place empty bottles in an insulated box on our front porch. The next morning, full ones were in their places. Twice weekly, I would lie awake until I heard the front door open and the clink of empty bottles being set outside, then slip from my bed to peer out my front window to make sure my parents didn't get in their car and drive off. I did this for as long as the dairy provided home delivery.

My fear of abandonment improved after I was married, but my stomach still knotted when Jerry left me alone with a pile of boxes in a basement apartment in the roll-up-the-sidewalks town of LaPlata, Maryland. Jerry moved into the basement apartment of my parents' home in Charlottesville.

I distinctly remember telling Jerry that there was a reason we were going to work in different states. When my father became ill during the fall of 1975, I was sure our separation was so that Jerry would be available to transport my disabled mom daily to and from the hospital and later the nursing home. After my father's death on February 29, 1976, Jerry became my mom's lifeline, helping her settle my dad's estate and taking her to various meetings related to it. Truthfully, I don't know what she would have done without Jerry there to assist her. But there is more; God had something in mind for me, too.

Mrs. Bakersfield was an aide in the classroom next to mine during that first year of teaching. She was a dear Christian woman whose profound witness brought me very close to the Lord. One night during dinner at her home, she told me the story of her daughter, who for several months had complained that her skirt alternately got too loose or tight. She said that she would move the button back and forth on her daughter's skirt repeatedly. Then her daughter was diagnosed with leukemia.

In those days, this diagnosis was a death sentence. Her daughter died at the age of nine. Mrs. Bakersfield shared that she wept all of her tears over her daughter's death and had never again shed a tear, not even when her husband passed away. In spite of this great tragedy, her faith was unshakeable. Daily she saw God's hand in every aspect of her life, and she had absolute confidence that she would see her beloved daughter again.

As I watched and learned from her, I realized that I wanted faith like hers, too. So, one night in the quietness of my little basement apartment, I asked the Lord into my life. Mind you, I had attended church all of my life and had confessed my faith when I joined the church at age twelve. I certainly felt a relationship with the Lord. But on this night, my relationship changed. It became fuller, more energized, alive. It would become the rock on which to stand when the rest of my world crumbled beneath me. Thank you, Lord.

The following year, Jerry and I were very relieved when Augusta County Schools hired me as a teacher, and we moved into a small rental home in the Shenandoah Valley.

Within a week of the first visit to the pediatrician, I took Emily to our family doctor, hoping that he might have the answer to her worsening condition. Friends and family, including Bubbles, had already suggested that Emily's illness might be "in her head."

Jerry and I had discussed the possibility and felt strongly that it was *not* in her head. To my surprise, almost immediately Dr. Massey began to delve into the possibility of an emotional component.

"Are things okay at home? How is Emily getting along in school? Is anything bothering her? Could she be pregnant?"

"Could she be pregnant?" I was stunned. Never had this thought occurred to me. "Emily, pregnant?" The words banged in my head while my face turned red with embarrassment and anger. "Not Emily. She's only twelve."

With a look of understanding and mild bewilderment, he replied, "If this were my daughter, I would do a pregnancy test. In this day, you never know what your children are doing."

"Jerry," I said when Emily and I returned home, "he thinks she might be pregnant. I gave him permission to run the test, but she doesn't know."

A cloud born from the wisdom of counseling children and youth for many years crossed over Jerry's face. "When will we know?" he asked.

"Soon," I responded.

"You know," Jerry said, "they don't know so they have to run all the tests. That is all it is."

Even though I was shocked by Dr. Massey's line of questioning and its implications for Emily, I found myself wondering about her lifestyle. I thought I knew her well. I took her to dance classes, school dances, friends' houses for sleepovers, and Little League cheerleading practice. I listened to her idle chatter while riding in the car. I attended teacher conferences. Never was there any hint that my innocent little twelve-year-old might have a secret life. I felt desperate, scared, and really humiliated.

Emily, who possessed a remarkable ability to read people, including her mother, asked me the next day what test the doctor had ordered. Deciding to be honest, I said that he was running a pregnancy test. With a mortified look on her face, she blurted out, "But, Mom, I don't even have a boyfriend!"

The weekend of January 7–9 saw a dramatic decline in Emily's condition. She would drink nothing but Kool-Aid. When it reached her stomach, it bubbled and boiled. The noise, which could be heard across the room, sounded like liquid being poured from a bottle. No longer able to make it to the bathroom, she draped herself over the kitchen garbage can as she waited for the inevitable. Like some precision machine, within seconds of taking a sip of liquid, the drink was ejected from her body. Helpless, all I could do was rub her back and stomach. Ann wept at her sister's suffering.

On Saturday night, as Emily lay still on the couch, too ill even to watch television, I looked at her pale face. I could no longer discern color between her lips and cheeks. She looked dead. I was terrified. "Please, God," I prayed silently over her, "let the doctors find out what is wrong. Let it be soon."

By Monday I was ready to demand that Emily be hospitalized until whatever she had could be identified and treated. I made another appointment with Dr. Massey for twelve thirty that afternoon. I called Jerry and asked him to meet us at the doctor's office, thinking his presence would add extra clout to my demands. I was absolutely desperate for an answer; something had to be done. We met at the appointed hour. Emily tried to stretch out on the examination table, but she was in too much pain to lie flat. Before the doctor could examine her belly, she vomited. The intense pain in her stomach was too obvious to ignore. There could be no mistake; Emily was very ill.

Before admitting her to Staunton's King's Daughters' Hospital, Dr. Massey ordered another upper GI, but this time it would include a follow-through. Jerry, who is so often right, had already said to me that they weren't looking low enough. He was right again. An intestinal blockage was found in Emily's gut near her appendix.

Suddenly the nausea made perfect sense. Why didn't anyone think of an intestinal blockage three weeks earlier?

In late afternoon, Emily was taken to her hospital room. The first order of business was to place a nasogastric (NG) tube through her nose into her stomach to allow the blocked fluids to drain. This couldn't be happening. My own gut screamed that things were serious. I broke down in tears as I left Emily to the nurses who would guide the tube through her nose and into her stomach.

When Jerry and I returned to her room a few minutes later, the tube exiting her nose and already pouring green liquid into a container, she stated in a matter-of-fact way, "It wasn't so bad." By that night, a copious amount of fluid had drained and she felt much better. We rejoiced that for the first time in days, Emily had gone more than thirty minutes without vomiting.

Word of Emily's hospitalization spread quickly. Soon balloons, cards, and flowers began to arrive. We were encouraged to hear Dr. Massey say that he hoped and expected the blockage to unkink naturally as the pressure in her intestines was lessened. He asked if Emily had ever had abdominal surgery, which could cause scar tissue and a blockage.

"No," I replied, not aware of the implications of my response. "Her only surgery was to remove her adenoids several years ago." I felt a sense of calm that I had not known for weeks. I felt vindicated that she was not suffering from some unrecognized emotional trauma. Nor was she pregnant.

By Tuesday morning, Emily was feeling markedly better. I was amazed at the volume of dark green liquid that had collected in the container overnight. No wonder she was desperately ill. More x-rays were done; the blockage remained. A computer tomography (CT) scan was scheduled for Wednesday morning. In the meantime, Emily settled into her hospital room and did what came natural to her—endearing herself to the pediatric nursing staff. She called them by name and babbled lots of adolescent nonsense, making them laugh. She watched television to her heart's content.

The CT scan done on Wednesday showed that not only was the blockage still present, an abnormality was found in the area of her appendix. As Dr. Massey had done earlier, the radiologist asked me if Emily had ever had any type of abdominal surgery. "No," I replied, "none at all." There was no vindication for me this time, just a churning deep in my belly.

Around the noon hour, Dr. Massey came by Emily's room. He said that he suspected her appendix had ruptured at some point and walled itself off. He had a long medical term for it, but I can't remember what it was. He said he had talked to local surgeons and, because of Emily's age, they felt she should be seen by a pediatric surgeon at the University of Virginia Hospital. He had already made arrangements for an ambulance to transport her the thirty-five miles to Charlottesville. He wanted us to leave as soon as possible.

Suddenly things were happening with lightning speed. I called Jerry at work to tell him to meet me in Charlottesville. Little did he know that when he left work that day, he would not return for the next five weeks. A neighbor came to stay with Emily while I dashed home to explain to my mom what was happening and to toss a few essentials into a suitcase.

I quickly returned to the hospital and watched two ambulance attendants load Emily onto a gurney. They wrapped her in three or four white blankets until only her freckled face was visible. The NG tube was clamped off, but the ugly brown hose still exited her nose, which had begun to itch from the tape that held the tubing in place. Emily pulled her hand from her blanket cocoon so she could give a royal wave as she rolled past the nurses' station. She was smiling as usual. You would have thought she was off to a party rather than to another hospital.

Within minutes, she was secured in the ambulance. I climbed into the front seat and watched the driver flip on the overhead emergency lights. I wondered if the siren would also blare. I felt an overwhelming sense of panic at that moment. The events of the past two hours seemed completely impossible. I knew that only the sickest people were sent to UVA for treatment. It was January 12, 1994.

Lessons from Emily

Chapter 2

I have cancer.
I used to be a dancer.
Now I have a problem with my bowel.

—excerpt from a poem
written by Emily,
May 1994

The journey to Charlottesville seemed interminable. Traffic was forced to a crawl through thick fog that blanketed both sides of Afton Mountain, which, as part of the ancient Blue Ridge Mountains, separated the beautiful Shenandoah Valley from the Piedmont region of Virginia. I listened with half an ear as the driver made light conversation. Mostly, though, my mind churned with questions about what lay ahead of us. How much school would Emily miss? How long before she could dance again? How dangerous would her surgery be? Emily, oblivious to the fog and idle chatter, slept for most of the trip.

After arriving at the Emergency Room of the University of Virginia Health System, we were passed from one station to another on our journey to the seventh floor. We would later learn that the seventh floor was known as the Children's Medical Center, or CMC. It was soon to become our second home.

Emily was assigned to a semiprivate room and, within minutes, had mastered the system of buttons to flip through television channels and adjust her bed. She called Bubbles right away to let her know she had arrived safely. She gave an account of her new surroundings as though she'd just checked into a hotel. Preschool chatter could be heard coming from the little girl in the bed on the other side of the curtain. I settled into the large, blue-vinyl parent chair that sat between Emily's bed and the window. The room felt strangely dark, rather like I was in a tunnel. There was light at the end of the tunnel, though; it was florescent and shone right above Emily's bed.

I looked out the window at the city surrounding the hospital. A freight train rumbled slowly west on the tracks that were adjacent to the building. Soon after, Jerry arrived, and I felt an enormous sense of relief. Jerry and I had married in December 1972. Now more than twenty-one years later, he was still my best friend and the one person who could steady my course when stress threatened to overtake my ability to reason.

I wondered how single parents managed the hospitalization of a child, especially if other children had to be left at home, such as in our case. How grateful I felt that my situation allowed my husband to join me, while my mother, who by this time had lived with us for more than ten years, would be home for Ann, who was now a sophomore in high school.

Emily had been in her room only a short while when I heard a voice coming from the hallway that I thought I recognized. As coordinator of special education programs at my school, I had had phone contact with an educational consultant from the Hospital Education Program (HEP) who followed one of my students in an outpatient clinic. Ginger Ellingwood's voice and laugh were unmistakable. Before I knew it, she and her TV crew popped into our room to invite Emily to participate in the HEP's closed-circuit television production called *Confetti*, a bingo-type game designed to help patients learn medical terminology.

Emily, who was not known to be particularly shy, could not be persuaded to go to the hospital studio. She did agree to call in an answer to a riddle that Ginger would ask on camera. Promptly at 3:30 p.m., we tuned our room television to Channel 12 and joined in *Confetti*. Ginger asked her riddle, but Emily, now too shy even to call in, convinced her dad to do it for her. Never shy, Jerry complied and had a funny little conversation with Ginger. They've been great friends ever since.

Two weeks later, Emily, surrounded by a group of hometown friends, went to the studio to play *Confetti* live for the first time. She and her friends had fun. The HEP gave me a copy of the show, which became the first volume in our video library of Emily's Hospital Adventures.

Shortly after seven o'clock that night, a young surgeon, Dr. Eugene McGahren, and his team of residents and medical students entered the room. They were friendly and articulate, joking about my cooking, which, they said, *must* have triggered Emily's gastrointestinal difficulties. We laughed and listened as they continued to talk to Emily, teasing her about boyfriends and questioning her about school, building in her and in us a sense of security and trust. Within minutes they were gone, and we were left to marvel at the sheer number of eager young doctors, relaxed and confident in this setting, who had come to meet our Emily.

Perhaps an hour or so later, Dr. McGahren returned to the room. This time he was alone, and his face was more serious. He sat at the foot of Emily's bed and began to talk with us about the CT scans that he had reviewed earlier. With experience in his voice, he gently explained that the CT scans showed an abnormality in Emily's intestine. This *growth*, he said, was most likely not the result of a ruptured appendix. Jerry, whose wisdom superseded my own naiveté, stated, "You mean as in cancer?"

Dr. McGahren quietly said, "Yes, I think Emily has cancer."

As I sat in the parent chair, my head reeling from the poisoned word-arrow newly plunged into my heart, I remember looking at Emily. She had leaned back in her bed, hands folded behind her head. She did not have the first look of concern on her face. Rather, she looked peaceful.

"Oh, God, Emily," I thought to myself, "You have cancer." Like a caged lioness, I wanted to bolt from the confining walls of her hospital room. Never in my life had I felt such complete panic. Not even when Dr. McGahren said that he suspected Emily had non-Hodgkin's lymphoma, a treatable cancer with a 95 percent cure rate in children, did the terror in me subside.

When Dr. McGahren left the room moments later, I left, too. I could not bear to be with Emily as the uncontrollable cries erupted from the depths of my soul. I could not bear to see her face, serene and sweet, without a trace of fear. Outside her room, my face buried in my hands, mammoth sobs poured forth from the deepest places of my heart. Even a stranger's tender arms around my heaving shoulders, her soft whispers of comfort in my ear, brought no relief from the raging anguish in my spirit.

Emily, who had returned to watching television, noticed Jerry was also crying. In her typical, direct manner, she looked at him and asked, "Daddy, why are you crying?"

"Dr. McGahren thinks you might have cancer," he replied. "That is a very hard thing for parents to hear, because cancer is a very serious illness."

Emily, who did not want to see anyone crying, simply returned to watching her television show. She continued to watch television that evening. She never asked any more questions of us or shed a single tear. And from that point on, whenever Jerry needed to cry, he left the room.

When at last I returned to Emily's room, my body drained of tears, we sat in silence for a short while, each of us looking at the television, only Emily watching it. Jerry and I agreed with Dr. McGahren's plan to operate as soon as possible. First, however, more tests were necessary. They were scheduled for the following day.

For the next few minutes, a stream of medical professionals came to Emily's room, explaining hospital protocol and providing us with a broad scope of cancer treatments. Emily's specific treatment plan would be tailored to a final diagnosis, which would be determined by pathology. We were encouraged to remain positive and reminded that lymphoma had an excellent cure rate. Though I forced a weak smile in response, inwardly, feelings of dread consumed me. When at last the three of us were alone, I felt trapped and claustrophobic again. Desperate to get away, I called local friends to request the use of their shower and a phone to make calls out of Emily's hearing.

"Caroline, how nice to hear from you. Why, yes. Come right on out. We'd love to have you," my friend Bobbie Mooney said, her wonderful Charlottesville accent exuding southern hospitality.

And so, for the first time in days, I left Emily. As I drove away from the hospital, in my mind I recounted the previous week, astounded by all that had happened. Hours and days were blurred together strangely. Could it be that just a month ago Emily was a regular kid with a regular life, dancing and decorating her way through the holiday season?

Just as a thick fog had settled on the city of Charlottesville that night, making it impossible to see more than a few yards beyond my headlights, so had a thick fog settled on Emily's future, making it impossible to guess what lay ahead for her. By the power of a six-letter word, our lives had been changed forever.

Having driven the five or so miles north of Charlottesville to the entrance of my friends' farm, I crept slowly up the long driveway, straining to see the gravel lane through the dense fog. Suddenly, a large herd of deer appeared directly in front of me. They stood motionless in the blinding glare of my headlights. For an instant they reminded me of Emily, wide-eyed and beautiful. Then, in the blink of an eye, they disappeared into the milky night. How I longed for my own nightmare to do the same—to vanish so that not even a memory remained.

Once inside the Mooneys' warm and welcoming home, I could not hold back my sobs as my longtime friends gave me kind words of comfort. "Emily is a big, strong girl," Russell said. "They have all kinds of new treatments these days. She's going to be just fine."

"I know, I know," I said to myself, trying to smile. But the dread would not leave me.

Following a soothing shower, I began making the phone calls that I did not want Emily to hear. First I called my mom to let her know what Emily had not shared earlier. Hearing the panic in my voice, she was adamant: "Caroline," she stated, "you have to be strong for Emily. She needs you now more than ever. Everything will be all right. We'll pray. God will stand by you. Emily will be all right."

Next I called Ann, the secretary at my school. Ann's daughter, Katie, and Emily had been best friends for several years. Again the sobs took away my ability to talk. "Ann, the doctors at UVA think Emily has cancer. She needs surgery. Please don't tell Katie. I don't know when I'll be back at school," I finally managed to get out.

I could hear Ann forcing back her own tears. She assured me that all my duties would be covered at school, and she promised not to tell Katie. We talked for a few more minutes before I prepared to dial others who needed to know what was happening.

Many years later, Ann shared that when her son, Daniel, who was a few years older than Emily, heard about her cancer diagnosis, he broke down in tears. "It's not fair, Mom. She's just a teenager."

When I returned to the hospital, I found Emily and Jerry much as I had left them, although they both seemed engrossed in a television show. I wondered how they could be so calm. Realizing we had not eaten in hours, Jerry and I decided to go to the hospital cafeteria to get some dinner. So mundane an act as selecting food was nearly impossible for us, however. As we stared at the available entrees, we seemed unable to make a decision. A hollow numbness had robbed us, not only of our ability to think but also of our appetites.

Over the next two weeks, this scenario would be played out repeatedly in various settings where making even the simplest decision challenged us. Numbness, we slowly recognized, was the first wave of the mental and emotional war waged against parents of children with cancer.

As promised, Thursday was filled with presurgery tests: x-rays of Emily's chest and belly, an ultrasound, blood work. In the evening, Dr. McGahren told us that her surgery was scheduled for the next day. He and the surgical team would remove the bowel obstruction, a procedure that might mean actually removing a section of her bowel. During surgery, he would also check her ovaries, which, on scans, were abnormally large.

As we would soon learn, modern medicine not only allowed but encouraged active participation by the pediatric patient in many medical decisions. In accordance with this philosophy, prior to Emily's surgery, we were asked to help her choose a method of central line, or catheter, which would be buried in her chest and used for chemotherapy treatments. Along with Jerry and me, Emily listened attentively as a nurse explained in layman's terms the two basic types of catheter. Together we chose a port-a-cath. It would be placed completely under Emily's skin, thus allowing her to swim and enjoy herself in the summer months without visible tubes running out of her chest. The chance for serious blood infections would be diminished with the use of a port-a-cath, as well.

We expected Emily to be taken into surgery early Friday afternoon. Due to operating room delays, however, she was not taken to the pediatric induction room until five fifteen that evening. Once there, she received medicines that relaxed and calmed her. An hour later, when she was called into surgery, she left us laughing and joking with the nurses and doctors. Once out of her sight, Jerry and I wept, not only at the dread of learning about her cancer, but also at the strength and will of our child.

Dr. McGahren had prepared us to expect Emily's surgery to last several hours. Every hour or so, a nurse or doctor came to us in the surgery waiting room to brief us on events taking place in the OR. Early in the evening, other families sat in tight groups waiting for news of their loved ones. Gradually, however, all the people left. By midnight, Jerry and I were alone in the waiting area. Shortly after midnight, a young doctor, Laurel Rice, came out to speak with us. Dr. Rice was a gynecologist/oncologist.

"How are you guys doing?" she asked, looking into our exhausted eyes. Her smile was warm and her voice was friendly, but her next words cut straight to the issue. "Emily's cancer is very unusual. I think she has ovarian cancer, but we won't know until pathology confirms it."

"You mean Emily doesn't have lymphoma?" I asked, stunned.

"Without a pathology report, we can't tell what kind of cancer she has," Dr. Rice gently explained, "but I think it is ovarian. Ovarian cancer is rare in a patient as young as Emily, but it does occur, and it is treatable." After giving us a few more words of encouragement, she disappeared back into the OR. The sickening dread returned to my stomach as the *hope* of lymphoma and its 95 percent cure rate evaporated from my thinking.

In another hour or so, a drained and grim Dr. McGahren emerged from the OR to meet with us. He told us that Emily definitely had cancer, but he was totally baffled by the type. He described her cancer as hundreds of tiny nodules, something like small cherries, about the size of the end of one's little finger, peppering her intestines, uterus, and other abdominal organs. Her ovaries, he said, were badly cancerous. Emily's surgery was lengthy, not because the bowel resection was difficult, but because the pathologists kept asking for tissue samples as they struggled to determine the type of cancer. Unable to come to a decision, Dr. McGahren had opted to close the incision and wait for a later diagnosis.

In an effort to leave us with some encouragement, Dr. McGahren said that the bowel obstruction itself had been removed easily and that Emily would feel much better once she had recovered from the surgery. Finally, he said that we would be allowed to join her in the recovery room in a short while. Someone from recovery would call us on the house phone to let us know when and where. Then he was gone. Jerry and I were alone in the family waiting room. We waited and waited, but no call came telling us we could go to Emily.

Feeling anxious that she might awaken, frightened without her parents nearby, we decided to try to find her on our own. It was then that we experienced what we believe was our first "little" miracle, for there, walking down a deserted corridor at one fifteen in the morning, was a hospital chaplain.

"May I help you?" she asked kindly, obviously seeing the stress and exhaustion on our faces.

"Yes, you can," we replied simultaneously. "Our daughter has had surgery and is in the recovery room, but we don't know how to get there."

"I'll be happy to take you," she said. And thus began a precious and supportive friendship that extended over many months.

❧

Never having been in the recovery room of a large teaching hospital, I looked around me with some curiosity as we entered the Post Anesthesia Care Unit, or PACU. There were spaces for, perhaps, fifteen or twenty patients—no walls, just curtains to be pulled for privacy. There were warming lamps, monitors, and IV hangers dangling from the ceiling for every patient station. Numerous cabinets lined the walls, each holding IV solutions and other supplies needed for recovering patients.

During a routine day, the PACU would be vibrant with activity as doctors, nurses, technicians, and, in the case of children, loved ones huddled around slowly waking patients. Now, at one thirty, the PACU was eerily quiet—except for the soft moans that could be heard coming from the only patient in the room.

While not asked to wear masks, we were asked to robe ourselves in yellow hospital gowns before going to Emily's bedside. Slipping into them as quickly as possible, we noticed that they actually felt good, since the temperature in the recovery room was quite cool. Walking around to her bed, I felt my eyes burn with tears as I saw my sweet child, tubes running from every direction, monitors buzzing and beeping as they kept track of her vital signs.

Soft, hoarse moans slipped between her badly chapped lips as tears inched from her half-opened eyes. I wanted desperately to cradle her in my arms, to whisper to her that soon the pain would go away. With Jerry on one side and me on the other, however, all we could do was stroke her face and tell her how much we loved her.

We remained in the recovery room with Emily for another thirty minutes or so until she was stable enough to be taken to her hospital room. At two fifteen on Saturday morning, we returned to 7 Central. There Emily was gently moved from the hard gurney to her bed. Her vital signs were once again checked, and then she was able to rest quietly for the remainder of the night with only occasional interruptions for temperature and blood pressure checks. I curled up in the parent chair, and Jerry slept on the sofa in the dayroom at the end of the hall.

Even before the Saturday sun inched above the horizon, Dr. Rice slipped quietly into Emily's room. She seemed pleased with Emily's progress postoperatively. Speaking to us outside Emily's room, she told Jerry, who looked absolutely terrible, never to forget to eat and sleep. He never forgot her advice.

Dr. Rice remained convinced that Emily's cancer was ovarian. Later that morning, another pediatric cancer specialist, Dr. Pedro De Alarcon, stopped by to see us. I remember that he had a cold, and he wore a mask over his mouth and nose. Seeing only his eyes, we listened as he cautioned us that only a *final* pathology report would yield the truth of Emily's cancer. Until we had that report, no one could positively identify the cancer within her.

While this message was given to us consistently by all the doctors, Jerry and I found it difficult not to cling to the opinions that offered the most hope. It was obvious, however, that Emily's condition was mysterious and had opened up many questions in the world of childhood cancer.

Trust in the Lord with all your heart

and lean not on your own understanding.

—*Proverbs 3:5*

As the morning gave way to the afternoon, we could see that Emily looked much better. Her color was good and she was more alert, though she complained of her back hurting a great deal. Not only had she been on the operating table for more than six hours, a bone marrow test had been conducted to see if there were cancer cells in her blood. The site of this test was near her lower back and very likely contributed to the intensity of her pain. She didn't get much relief until we sandwiched her between six pillows. She failed to see the humor of looking like a graham cracker between two marshmallows.

Because the medical staff at the University of Virginia Hospital elected to treat pain very aggressively, Emily's doctor ordered a pain pump for her to use postoperatively. This miracle box allowed Emily to give herself morphine as she needed it. I have a very high tolerance for pain, so watching her self-medicate made me a bit uncomfortable. Not Emily. She pushed the button over and over again until she reached a level of comfort suitable to her.

During the day, many of Emily's friends and family came to see her. At her request, we did not turn on lights or open the blinds. It was not unusual for her friends to leave the room visibly upset. Understandably, it was difficult to see Emily in pain and with tubes, IVs, and pumps helping sustain her. Without fail she wanted to know who of her visitors cried. Whatever her thoughts were, she kept them to herself.

Late that afternoon, during a lull between visitors and in the darkness of her room, Emily, struggling to get comfortable, suddenly looked at her dad and me and said, "I don't know why this had to happen to me." And with her very next breath she said, "But I wouldn't want anybody else to have to go through this."

Concerning her cancer, those were the only words of complaint *ever* uttered by Emily to us. At that moment, I realized that this twelve-year-old child, who loved to dance and who, more than anything else, wanted to be a teacher, had already begun sharing her lessons.

Chapter 3

Keep your faith in the Lord
and you will be just fine.

—excerpt from a letter written
by Emily to a friend,
October 27, 1994

During the first nights of Emily's hospitalization in Charlottesville, Jerry and I both stayed there with her. My bed was the pullout parent chair in Emily's room, and Jerry slept on the sectional couch in the seventh floor dayroom. On Saturday, after we knew that Emily was stable, Jerry, on the recommendation of a nurse, got a room at the Ronald McDonald House (RMH). Located just a few blocks from the hospital, it was visible from the dayroom windows. The hospital shuttle made a stop there, we were told, making transportation available even when bad weather was a problem. We found comfort in knowing that, not only did we have a place to go for quiet, we had a soft, clean bed when needed.

Before Jerry left that night, we were given the wonderful news that Emily's bone marrow test was clear. As I lay down on my pullout bed around midnight, I gave thanks to God for that miracle. I also thanked God for the miracles that were to come. I remember whispering one of my favorite scriptures that night—Isaiah 53:5:

"But he was pierced for our transgressions, he was crushed for our iniquities; the punishment that brought us peace was upon him, and by his wounds we are healed."

Bright sunshine and bitter cold greeted us on Sunday morning. Jerry arrived around nine thirty, and we decided to give Emily some downtime while we went to the cafeteria for breakfast. To my surprise and delight, Jerry looked and sounded remarkably better than he had twenty-four hours earlier, proving Dr. Rice's sage advice to eat regularly and get plenty of sleep.

A short while later, we returned to Emily's room and learned that her doctors had decided that her NG tube could be removed, since she was doing so well. Emily was not yet ready for liquids, but removing the uncomfortable tube was an exciting first step toward health and healing.

For reasons unknown, she was reticent to allow her nurse to pull out the tube. Perhaps it had become a guarantee that she would no longer throw up or develop a blockage. Regardless of the reason, Emily and her nurse negotiated for a good while before she agreed for the tube to be removed. Over the months to come, she would perfect the art of negotiation, not only with the nurses but with her doctors and parents.

Once I knew that Emily was comfortable, Jerry took me to the RMH so I could take a nap. I remember how quiet Jerry's small room seemed. The bed was soft and warm, and I quickly drifted into a deep, refreshing sleep. I awoke five hours later, eager to return to Emily's hospital room.

In spite of the cold, a steady stream of visitors came to see Emily that afternoon. Dear Jerry spent all day patiently recounting recent events for each new set of visitors. Our Ann was among the first to arrive. For her, seeing Emily was important. In the span of seven days, our lives had been turned upside down. Hearing Emily's voice and seeing her smile proved that our world had not completely imploded.

By the close of visiting hours, a total of twenty-four friends and family members had braved the cold to visit Emily. Her bedside table and the window ledge were piled high with cards and gifts. She was exhausted yet energized by the love and care that enveloped her that day. As the seventh floor halls became quiet for the night, Emily sat in her bed, glancing occasionally at the television while contentedly playing with a favorite new gift—a Game Boy—given to her by Shannon, the daughter of Jerry's sister, Carol, and Carol's husband, Sam.

The Monday after Emily's surgery, the weather turned miserably cold. Sleet fell throughout most of the day. Unlike the weekend, when her bedside had been crowded with visitors, on this dreary day only doctors and nurses stopped by. Late in the afternoon, a chief surgeon paid a visit and announced that Emily needed to get out of bed and do a little walking.

Still very sore and relying heavily on the pain pump, she was not very interested in complying. Time to negotiate. If she would walk a short distance today, he coaxed, tomorrow she could have clear liquids. That motivated Emily, and, with her dad and me supporting her and a nurse walking behind her, she inched the few feet from her bed to the door and back. The eight-inch incision, which stretched from below her waist downward, was tight, and it was difficult for her to stand straight.

Dr. McGahren would tell us later that he had been impressed with the firmness of Emily's abdominal muscle wall. "She's a dancer," Jerry and I replied almost in unison. The baby steps taken late that Monday signaled a milestone in her recovery. We believed the worst was behind us.

With Emily's permission, that night I joined Jerry at the Ronald McDonald House. For the first time in what seemed like months to me, I slept well. Tuesday morning was bitterly cold. The sleet and rain that had fallen the day before had turned to solid ice. We were grateful for the shuttle that transported us to the hospital at around ten o'clock. Emily was waiting for us, propped up in bed, watching television. "That nurse jerked me around, and it hurt," she fussed. "Tonight, Momma, you're going to stay here." And that marked the end to my nights at the RMH.

Later in the morning, Dr. Kim Dunsmore, who was Emily's primary cancer doctor, stopped by to tell us that CT scans of her head, chest, and abdomen had been ordered to determine if the cancer had spread. Emily struggled to drink three cups of dye in preparation for the scans. She vomited twice, but we knew that was caused by a reaction to the dye rather than by a blockage.

Sometime after ten that night, we were told that the scans were good. Emily's chest was clear, and her abdomen was as they expected it to be. The result of the head scan would not be available until the next day. Again I praised Jesus for the gift of a clear chest. In my heart I knew her brain was also free of cancer. Reports the next day confirmed my thoughts.

We asked daily about a report from pathology, but none was yet available. We were told that a blood sample had been sent away to check for markers for an ovarian tumor, but the results from that test would not be available for several days. How many times had we heard that it is the waiting that is the hardest part of a serious illness? Determined to remain positive with Emily, only in the private pages of my journal did I confess my frustration:

Wait. Wait. Wait. Maybe tomorrow.

We can only hope.

Tuesday, January 18, 1994

The following day brought little change in the weather and no news of the pathology report, although during his regular rounds,

Dr. McGahren told us that we should plan on a late-afternoon meeting the next day with the full team of doctors. Hearing the word *meeting* made my stomach flip. Knowing that Emily's future rested in the hands of a group of pathologists was unnerving. The course of her life depended on their decision.

Early in the afternoon of January 19, Emily's morphine pump was discontinued. Within several hours, Jerry and I began to see a transformation as her body was released from the effects of the drug. While on morphine, Emily was sluggish and subdued, often teary and difficult. Taking even short walks challenged her as much emotionally as physically. Even though it was painful for her, we inwardly rejoiced to hear her laugh ever so softly, for her giggles signaled the return to her natural humor. With renewed energy, she accepted the challenge to walk as much as possible and within a day hiked to and from the nurses' station, the dayroom, and the hospital school.

Sometime during the afternoon, Dr. McGahren met with Jerry and me to discuss the possibility of removing Emily's badly cancerous ovaries. They were enlarged and would likely cause her pain. We agreed that, even though she was just now recovering from the first surgery, this second surgery would benefit her. So Emily was scheduled for another abdominal surgery exactly one week following her first operation.

We were still processing the fact that a second major surgery was ahead of us when our minister at Central United Methodist Church and his wife, Hugh and Sharon Harris, came into Emily's room. Hugh had a strong healing ministry and often spoke words of comfort at just the right moment. After chatting for a bit, they asked each of us for what we would have them pray. I said, quite simply, "Peace." I could not find it in my heart to ask for prayers for healing. All I wanted now was peace that only God could provide. I had inwardly longed for His peace since Emily's illness first began but had not really found it.

Jerry asked for peace, joy, and strength.

With a sweet sincerity, Sharon said, "All right, Caroline. We'll ask for His peace. And Jerry, we'll ask for peace, joy, and strength for you."

Regretfully, neither Jerry nor I can remember Emily's request.

During the evening, Emily began to experience severe cramping in her abdomen. Frightened that something was wrong, we quickly called a nurse, who listened to Emily's belly. To our considerable relief, Emily's gut was "waking up" from surgery. With the blockage removed she was on the verge of passing gas. How sweet the sound! With an enthusiasm not seen in weeks, she sat in her hospital bed and worked on school assignments for several hours. Life was beginning to feel a little bit normal—a gift of extraordinary proportion.

> He will cover you with his feathers,
>
> and under his wings you will find refuge;
>
> his faithfulness will be your shield and rampart.
>
> —Psalm 91:4

As with Emily's first surgery, presurgery abdominal x-rays were needed. These were scheduled for Thursday morning, the day before the surgery. We had grown accustomed to frequent trips to the x-ray lab and knew their routines well. Stretching flat on the table was difficult for Emily for these films. The technicians were sympathetic to her complaints and went the extra mile to find pillows and blankets to help make her comfortable while the x-rays were taken.

Emily could not return to 7 Central until there was confirmation that the films were satisfactory. As we waited in the dim coolness of the room, I decided to talk to her about the surgery that would forever eliminate her ability to conceive a child. For years Emily had talked about how she would one day raise her own children. She was a no-nonsense sort of girl when given charge over younger children. She was adamant that *her* children would not be spoiled in any way. *Her* children would listen and respond to their mother's words.

She listened closely as I carefully and gently explained the implications of the second surgery to her. With wisdom that far outweighed my own, she said to me, "Oh, Mom, don't you know there are all sorts of children in the world who need adopting?"

I looked at her with awe and wonder. Shaking my head slowly, I softly replied, "Emily, you're exactly right."

If I had not realized it before, I recognized now with absolute certainty that this child of mine would not accept defeat. The cancerous mountains that lay before her were, in her eyes, only gentle, rolling hills.

Just as Dr. McGahren had indicated, at around five o'clock on Thursday afternoon, a group of doctors, nurses, and a social worker began to gather outside the conference room that was located just down the hall from Emily's room. Jerry, who had periodically scouted the hallway outside Emily's door, turned and said, "They're here." Trying to be upbeat, we told her that we were going to the meeting and would return as soon as possible.

Assembled around the conference room table were the men and women who would direct the course of Emily's life—Dr. Rice, ob/gyn oncologist; Dr. Dunsmore, pediatric oncologist; Dr. McGahren, pediatric surgeon; and Theresa Andrews, social worker. The atmosphere was dense and heavy as Dr. McGahren spoke of Emily's condition. He explained that her cancer was so rare that identifying it had caused much debate among the hospital pathologists. They had determined, however, that Emily had a form of cancer called adenocarcinoma of the small bowel, a cancer most often found in older adult males. She was, he thought, the youngest case ever recorded for this type of cancer. "Emily," he said, "has made medical history."

Then he told us the prognosis was not good. It would take a miracle for Emily to beat this cancer.

Jerry, always wise and always strong, asked questions of the doctors who sat around the table. They answered him with kind frankness, saying that a course of treatment was yet to be determined. The possibility existed, however, that, when Emily was strong enough, we might have to travel to St. Jude's Hospital in Memphis for additional tests and treatment.

For the second time since Emily's arrival at UVA, I could not stop the sobs that poured forth from my spirit. Dr. Rice, who had two young children of her own, came and put her arm around my shoulders, sharing with me a sadness that only a mother can understand, each of us acknowledging in silence the deadly, raging cancer that imprisoned Emily.

We felt a personal attachment to most of Emily's doctors, but Dr. Rice was special. She was a no-nonsense woman who always wore pearls. She even wore her pearls in surgery. She connected with Emily and, particularly, me from our first meeting. Dr. Rice and I are still friends.

Recognizing our devastation, the doctors offered to talk to Emily for us. As it happened, our older daughter, Ann, was visiting, too, and could be told the news at the same time if we preferred. Gratefully, we accepted their offer and were soon alone. Together Jerry and I held each other and wept with the realization that Emily's own childhood dreams, as well as our aspirations for her future, except for a miracle, lay shattered around her. The feeling of utter loss was suffocating. As the helplessness clawed its way into our hearts and minds, determined to destroy what strength and courage we had left, we wondered how we could face our daughter. How could we return her clear, brave stare when, in our eyes, she would see our broken hearts?

As if in answer to our anguish, Emily, in her most remarkable fashion, wrote in her journal that night:

> Today [I] was told about the Cancer and stuff. I cried for a
> minute. Everyone else cried a lot. I tried to cheer dad and

everyone else up. I don't like it when other people feel bad about me. So what, I have a little cancer. It isn't going to kill me. I'm not worried. Go [sic] bye.

Love,

Emily Jones

On the darkest of nights, our twelve-year-old daughter had, in fact, carried us through as if on the wings of an angel.

Friday morning brought no surprises. Emily was readied for her surgery and around ten o'clock was called to the pediatric induction room. Seeming to enjoy a drug-induced euphoria, Emily once again happily separated from us. As she was rolled down the hall toward the automatic doors of the OR, she smiled at us and said, her voice mimicking a television commercial, "I love this place!" Everyone who heard her burst out laughing, including Jerry and me.

Rather than stay in the family waiting area for Dr. McGahren's report following Emily's operation, Jerry and I returned to the seventh floor to assist the staff as they moved Emily's belongings into a private room. We were deeply grateful for the opportunity to get a private room. Emily, whom we often dubbed the queen of television, frequently kept late hours. We were concerned that our hospital lifestyle might be bothersome to any patient sharing a semiprivate room with us. Also, knowing we were facing probable long-term hospitalizations, we yearned for a room where we could function more easily as a family, rejoicing in the victories and absorbing the disappointments privately.

At about twelve thirty, Dr. McGahren came to meet with us in Emily's "new" room. He confirmed that the removal of her ovaries had been the correct choice. Then he told us that he had left her uterus so that, even though she could not contribute an egg to a pregnancy, she could carry a baby. Surprised by his words, I did not know how to interpret this news. Did he expect Emily to survive her cancer even though she would need a miracle to do so? With a hope I had not dared allow, I remembered the words spoken in Mark 10:27: "With man this is impossible, but not with God; all things are possible with God." A wellspring of hope stirred in my spirit.

Shortly after Dr. McGahren left, we went once again to the PACU where we could be with Emily as she awoke from her surgery. Unlike the week before, however, she quickly stabilized and was soon back on the seventh floor enjoying her new accommodations, made truly cheery with huge balloon bouquets and cards sent by friends, as well as classrooms full of thoughtful school children.

Possibly because she was awake more quickly, she was alert to a great deal more pain. She self-administered medication through her morphine pump until she was comfortable. Her vital signs remained stable throughout the day, and, even though she had a slight temperature, we felt confident that she was on the way to a complete recovery. In my journal I wrote:

> Sweet Emily, tonight your surgeries are behind you. Let us move ahead with the joy and wonder of your life.
>
> Friday, January 21, 1994

During the day on Friday, we were visited by several of the teachers from my school. One of them left a small bag containing several gifts for Emily. Not until that night did I remember the bag. When I opened it, I found an envelope addressed to the family. In it was a poem written by Joanne Lam, Emily's beloved fourth-grade teacher. It read:

The snowflakes
Falling from Heaven, Lord
Laying a soft white blanket
Across the outstretched land.
How in all of this beauty, Father
Are we to understand
Why one of Your sweet little children
Is hurting and sick
And struggling to be brave?

You say, "It's all right to ask 'Why'
If it eases your heart."
Thank you, Lord.
You say, "I know her pain
And that of her family."
Ah, yes, Your Child suffered too.
You say, "I love her dearly
And will protect her always."
I know, Father, for that is Your way.
You say, "Her strength and bravery
Are earthly blessings of heavenly gifts."
Yes, God, You give sufficiently for the day.
You say, "Look again,
Up into the snow-filled heavens."

Each single, separate snowflake
Comes to earth, and we know not its purpose,
Just like the children You send

Who fill our lives with joy and wonder.
We admire their beauty, love their presence,
And are grateful for the blessing of life itself.
Some snowflakes nourish a tree,
Cleanse a leaf, water an animal.
The purpose of a child of God
Is His to define.

And so, You teach us to love,
To just love each other
Like the simple purity of the snow itself
And to trust You with all of the rest.

You say, "Peace to you now."
I say, "Amen."

Love in Christ,
Joanne
January 20, 1994

As Jerry read aloud the beautiful words written by my friend and colleague, I was reminded of the prayer request we had made two evenings before. Both of us had asked for *peace.* Here, in words so gentle and loving, God had spoken directly to us: "Peace to you now." And so, by God's unending grace, it was done.

The tears we wept that night were, for the first time since Emily had become ill, tears of joy; they were tears that recognized that God's timing is perfect. We felt safe with the assurance that not only Emily, but each of us, stood sheltered by the powerful wings of God.

Chapter 4

I like my new name!

—Emily to her parents,
February 3, 1994

Possibly because her dad had gone back to Staunton to take care of business too long neglected, on Saturday night Emily was particularly restless and unable to sleep. Not having had her hair washed in days, she allowed Katherine, her favorite night nurse, to give her an early morning in-bed shampoo just in time for a six o'clock surprise visit from a special family friend.

David Motes and his wife, Sharon, had joined our church in the late 1970s, and we had quickly become friends. For a number of years, we co-led the church youth group. In 1980, when Jerry and I renewed our wedding vows, David and Sharon stood with us at the altar. The only other people in attendance were our pastor and his wife. David loved surprise visits. It was he who, in 1978, had fooled the maternity ward nurses by telling them he was our pastor so that he could be the first to meet our newborn daughter, as proud of Baby Ann as though she were his own.

Now, before sunrise, this same sweet man slipped into Emily's room to comfort our second born, as anguished over Emily as though she, too, were his own. Over the coming months, it would become increasingly difficult for David to visit her. Sometimes he would not be able to enter her room at all, choosing to remain outside, his eyes and his spirit too filled with emotion for him to speak.

Emily's recovery progressed as anticipated over the next several days. Minor delays occurred when she ran a temperature for a day or so and when her NG tube, which had been replaced following her surgery, failed to work properly for a short period of time. She sat in the parent chair several times each day for an hour or so. She took short walks up and down the halls.

Emily had a particular penchant for helium balloons. Nothing made her happier than when visitors came bearing a balloon in hand. She was thrilled when a hospital volunteer entered her room with a bouquet of balloons. When her balloons no longer floated, Emily insisted that they be deflated and stored. I have no idea how she planned to use them. Perhaps she thought she could paper one of her bedroom walls with the wonderful array of colors and well wishes printed on many of the balloons. Maybe she planned to use them as her seventh-grade science teacher had suggested—for wrapping paper.

Even now, almost every balloon she received is pressed smooth and folded in a large gift bag, just as she wanted them. For me, those balloons, nearly one hundred in all, symbolize Emily's buoyant spirit—a spirit that refused to be suppressed during a dark, frightening time.

By the Tuesday following her second surgery, Emily's "nose-hose," as we fondly called her NG tube, was removed again, and she was started on clear liquids. She left her room to go to the hospital school, but, because she did not feel well, stayed only a short while. Jerry, who had returned from his "business trip" to Staunton, had begun to work on insurance forms.

Remarkably, the previous May, Jerry had taken out additional insurance coverage (cancer and heart policies) on the four of us. I remember clearly the day he announced what he had done. My retort was that the extra premiums would impact our monthly take-home pay. When I questioned Jerry about his decision, he said that he just *felt* he should do it. Now, eight months later, this policy afforded us the financial stability to miss as much work as necessary so we could be with Emily.

I didn't recognize it then, but purchasing supplemental insurance was just one example of Jerry's response to the inner voice that had prepared him for Emily's cancer. I was soon to realize another.

During Emily's third week as a patient in the Children's Medical Center, Jerry continued to stay at the Ronald McDonald House. One morning he came over to the hospital, and I immediately saw in his face an excitement I had not seen before. I knew he had something important to tell me. We visited with Emily for a short while, then he and I went to the dayroom while she went to the hospital school. He began to share with me his experience from the night before.

During the twenty-two years of our marriage, I had never known Jerry to have trouble falling asleep. Even at the Ronald McDonald House, he had enjoyed decent sleep. The previous night, however, sleep eluded him. He lay awake, his mind uncommonly restless, when a memory buried for more than twelve years had suddenly surfaced. He had been reminded of an evening in mid-February when I was very pregnant with a child whose sex was unknown to us. We had a name for a girl but could not decide on one for a boy. On this particular evening, he was given a word of knowledge that a male child *must* be called Isaac. He was so excited, positive that Isaac was exactly the name we should select. I, on the other hand, was less than enthusiastic.

"Jerry," I had protested, "we can't name a son *Isaac*. Isaac Jones—he'll grow up to be a blues singer."

"Caroline, it's a great name!" Jerry had insisted.

"Jerry, I don't think so. Why can't we call him *James Alexander* like you'd always planned? Isn't that an 'old' name from the Jones family? Or what about *Charles Carter* after my dad? Remember the southern tradition to name the first son after the wife's father? I like the idea of calling him 'Carter.' *Isaac*, Jerry? No, I just don't think so."

Now, twelve years later on a night when he was too restless to sleep, Jerry had been shown why he felt so strongly that a male child should be named Isaac. More than four thousand years ago, Abraham had been called upon by God to sacrifice his son, Isaac, and thereby to walk a walk of uncommon faith. Jerry felt strongly that God was asking us to sacrifice our child and walk a walk of uncommon faith. God rewarded Abraham's faith, I told myself. At the last moment, God provided a ram as a sacrifice, and Isaac was spared. Would our faith be rewarded in the same, wonderful way? Was not Jesus himself the final, perfect sacrifice?

> Now I know that you fear God,
>
> because you have not withheld
>
> from me your son, your only son.
>
> —Genesis 22:12

At that moment, Jerry and I, facing one another across a table in the dayroom, held hands and opened our hearts to God in prayer, acknowledging that God was sovereign and His will was perfect. We entrusted to Him Emily's life—*whatever* the outcome should be—healing on Earth or healing in heaven. At the conclusion of that prayer, we were, for the second time in just a few days, flooded with peace so perfect that words cannot express it. "Emily-Isaac," we said together. "What a wonderful name!"

As soon as possible, we shared the story with Emily. She adored being called Emily-Isaac and took pleasure in telling how she got her special name. It was a name that stuck with her throughout her illness.

During the fall months before Emily became sick, I went to bed many nights worried about the state of our family. Ann was involved in many extracurricular activities at her school and was often away at sporting events or meetings. Emily danced several nights a week. When she wasn't dancing, she was involved in Little League cheerleading. That took up two nights a week plus Saturday ball games. I spent my free time chauffeuring Ann, Emily, and, sometimes, my mother to their commitments and appointments. Jerry, who for years had been friend, confidant, and chauffeur to many youth in the Staunton area, was busy nearly seven days a week with his own commitments. We rarely took the time to enjoy an evening meal together.

Feeling afraid that our family might become lost, as so many others had, to the trends of the '90s, I began to pray—night after night—that God would *bond* my family. "Please, God," I prayed in the stillness of my bedroom, "*bond* us together. Don't let us be pulled in so many directions."

Now, with Emily in the hospital having been diagnosed with a cancer so rare that no other child had ever had it, the memory of those prayers gnawed at me day and night, making me feel nervous and guilty. My conscience bothered me so much that I could not discuss it with Jerry. Finally, after hearing his wonderful Isaac story, I told him about my prayers. With too much knowledge in his voice, he said to me, "You'd better be careful what you pray for, because you just might get it."

I knew this was true, and I began to feel even more distraught. One day a picture popped into my mind. I could see myself at a carnival. Before me were bobbing plastic ducks—millions of them—representing every child in the history of the world. As I watched, the brightly painted birds floated slowly down an endless canal, moving from right to left. Suddenly a voice could be heard, "Let me see. I'll pick one child to suffer a deadly cancer."

And with those words, an armless hand came down from somewhere above me and picked up one of the bouncing ducks. When it was turned over, there, in bold letters, was the name:

EMILY CAROLINE JONES.

To most, Emily's cancer would seem a random act. *I* knew, however, that God had allowed it in response to my selfish prayers. I felt that because of me, Emily was suffering horribly. "Why," I asked myself, "did I ever pray those prayers? Why couldn't I have let our lives remain as they were? Why did I ask God to bond us?" I agonized.

It was not until several days later that I received my answer. Sometime during a restless night it came to me that God had *allowed* my family to go in many directions so that I would pray the prayer *in preparation* for what was coming. I realized that God had confirmed first to Jerry and then to me that, even though we were to walk a walk of uncommon faith, He had prepared the way for us. God knew *even before Emily's birth* that she would have cancer. As sweet as a soothing balm, the words of a psalm flooded over me:

> For you created my inmost being;
> you knit me together in my mother's womb.
> I praise you because I am fearfully and wonderfully made;
> your works are wonderful,
> I know that full well.
> My frame was not hidden from you
> when I was made in the secret place.
> When I was woven together in the depths of the earth,
> your eyes saw my unformed body.

All the days ordained for me were written in your book
before one of them came to be.

—Psalm 139:13–16

Truly, that night I *was* comforted in the knowledge that even
my prayers were a part of God's plan for our lives. As peace again
permeated my spirit, I began to sense that something very precious
was happening.

I knew absolutely that Emily's illness was not a random act.

On the same Tuesday that Emily's NG tube was removed, Dr.
McGahren told Jerry that the pathologists were no longer certain of
their original diagnosis. The next day, Dr. Dunsmore, Emily's primary pediatric oncologist, confirmed this when she said the debate
continued to center on a diagnosis of small bowel versus ovarian
cancer. To help finalize a diagnosis, slides of Emily's tumors were
sent to two institutions, St. Jude's in Memphis and Massachusetts
General in Boston. By that point, Emily had been hospitalized for
sixteen days and had undergone two major surgeries.

We were now at a standstill. The only absolute was the knowledge that an unidentified, dangerous cancer was growing within
Emily. Dr. Rice, who, along with the other doctors, understood our
frustration, put the predicament in precise terms: "We have *one*
chance to make a correct diagnosis. We have to be 100 percent sure
of the type of cancer in order to determine the treatment. As hard
as it is, we have to wait."

And so we did, but this time we had a sense of peace and joy
born of faith. God was at work, and His light had begun to shine.

Chapter 5

Am I going to be famous?

—question posed by Emily
to Dr. Dunsmore,
January 31, 1994

Thursday, January 27, dawned cold and cloudy. Sleet and ice fell throughout the day. In Emily's room on the seventh floor, however, excitement and anticipation stirred as she received the go-ahead for solid food. Thinking that she would devour her breakfast after having been denied food for so long, I was surprised when no amount of coaxing would entice her to eat even a small amount of food from her tray.

Jerry quickly came to her defense and warned me to back off. "Emily will eat when she's ready," he insisted. As usual, he was right. Later that day she went with us to the cafeteria, where she ordered a hot dog and managed to eat—and enjoy—about half of it.

Because Emily was eating and making steady progress following her surgery, the doctors felt she should go home for a weekend furlough while they awaited the results from the slides that had been sent to other institutions for second opinions. Emily was thrilled with the idea and soon began to make plans for her time away from the hospital, including a trip to a wig shop so she could pick out a suitable hairpiece to use after her own hair fell out during chemotherapy.

Several teenaged girls on the seventh floor who were well into their own chemotherapy treatments had shown Emily their wigs. She seemed almost excited as she perceived herself joining a somewhat elite group. She made certain that Jerry knew where the most popular wig shop was located and insisted that we make it our first stop on the way home.

By the next morning, Emily's appetite was remarkably improved, and she enjoyed a good breakfast. Because her IV had been disconnected the night before, she was able to take a full shower, including a hair wash. Once under the warm streams of water, she stood for a long time letting the water splash over her head and body, sometimes laughing at this simplest of pleasures. After her hair was dried, Emily seemed to be more radiant than ever before. Not only did her beautiful auburn hair shine, her cheeks and face were aglow with a renewed zest for life. For the first time in weeks, her eyes sparkled with the anticipation of going home.

Because Emily made her journey to the University of Virginia Hospital wearing only a hospital gown under the pile of blankets, we realized we would need to purchase clothes for her. Emily, who loved clothes with a passion and could concoct stunning outfits from the most unlikely possibilities, instructed us to go to her favorite clothes store—Gap—to make the purchase. With strict orders about style, Jerry and I left her that Friday evening and made our way through slushy Charlottesville streets to the mall and the Gap store where, at some expense, we bought her an outfit, including matching socks. We then visited a second store, where we purchased a pair of tennis shoes.

Looking back on that fun shopping experience, I am reminded of Emily's birth. Even though she was born a full ten days past her due date, she was a pipsqueak at just eighteen inches in length. To bring her home from the hospital, Jerry bought her a precious pink dress with a white collar. Tiny Emily was lost in that darling newborn dress and her size 0 shoes would not stay on her miniature feet. Now, twelve years later, we had purchased another "going home" outfit. The excitement we felt that day was no less than it had been so many years earlier.

After we returned to the hospital with new clothes in hand, all was ready for the weekend furlough. We could hardly wait for Saturday to arrive! As though to add to our excitement, Dr. McGahren, during his evening rounds, stopped by Emily's room. With an unmistakable sincerity in his voice, he confidently said to her, "We're going to beat this thing." My heart soared as I heard those wonderful words while my spirit drank in his optimism.

Even though we were going home only on a weekend furlough, still we had to take everything—flowers, balloons, cards, and toys—with us. Because she had accumulated so much, it took several trips to the van before we were actually ready to load Emily. Then, to the cheers and encouragement of the seventh floor nursing staff, we set off for home, knowing that all the staff were working to keep our lives as normal as possible. It was a really good feeling.

Once at the wig shop, the reality of the *need* for a wig bothered Emily. She tried on a number of styles and colors but seemed unable to find one that suited her. Emily then confessed her fear of being teased. The shop manager reassured her that not all customers were cancer patients. Wigs were quite popular with young and old alike, many of whom wore wigs by choice, not out of necessity. She told Emily that her decision to order the wig early was a wise one—before she lost her hair—so that it would be ready when needed. She said that some girls wore their wigs along with their real hair so that when their real hair was gone, most people would not notice the change.

Perhaps the most comforting statement made was that the wig would be styled exactly as *she* desired. Emily, always the fashion queen, was pleased. With relief on her face, she chose a style she "sort of" liked. While the wig was similar in color to her own hair, the texture lacked the softness of natural hair. Natural hair wigs were available, but the cost was prohibitive to us.

In the coming months, we would realize that the wig was more of a security blanket than a necessity in Emily's life. After she became comfortable with her baldness, she left "Cindy," as she called her wig, on its stand, claiming that it was hot and itchy, opting instead to wear a baseball cap. During the course of her cancer, Emily accumulated a large number of baseball caps. Her favorite, however, was the cap whose logo read *Champion*.

Having ordered the wig, we arrived home in Staunton later that afternoon. Ann and Bubbles had the house sparkling clean and neat. Hanging on the wall was a cheerful "Welcome Home" banner made by Ann. She had also decorated Emily's room with more posters and signs. During the afternoon, friends stopped by to visit and to bring even more gifts and cards.

While Bubbles read every one of the hundreds of cards sent to Emily, the remainder of the family watched the video, *Aladdin*. Jerry paid bills. We were once again a "normal" family doing those things we had always done. Bubbles, whose love for Emily was enormous, wrote in Emily's journal that night:

January 29, 1994

My Dearest Emily,

What joy to put my arms around you and see you for the first time since Jan. 10 at KDH [King's Daughters' Hospital]. You look so good and happy to be home. Every day—dozens of times a day—I say a prayer for you and the family. I know God is watching over you and giving you strength and healing. His love comes to all of us through loving, caring friends. "Thank you, Heavenly Father, that Emily is home tonight.

I love her so dearly. Amen." 8:30 p.m.

Your Grandma Bubbles

Emily *was* happy to be home. She laughed and ate and talked to her friends on the telephone. She watched her beloved television. That first night before I went to sleep, I thanked God for the simple blessing of sleeping in my house, in my bed, with my family nearby.

Our furlough plan was to stay at home until early Monday morning, when Emily was to be prepared for whatever chemotherapy would be indicated by her specific diagnosis. By noon on Sunday, however, tiny snowflakes—the kind that announce a measurable snowfall—were tumbling from the darkening sky. Jerry decided we should make a hasty return to Charlottesville, where we could spend the night at a hotel that was located just a block from the hospital. Even if the snow accumulated, we could walk if necessary to our nine o'clock clinic appointment.

With great haste we packed our bags, loaded the van, and prepared to make the trip back across the mountain. Because we didn't know when we might be home again, the good-bye hugs were a little tighter and the good-bye kisses lasted a little longer.

At Emily's request, before leaving Staunton, we stopped by Taco Bell for a ten-pack of soft tacos. Then we dropped off some rented movies. At last, with snow falling fairly heavily, we headed for Charlottesville. Our furlough had lasted just twenty hours, but such a wonderful twenty hours they were!

Jerry checked us in to the hotel and, because it was Super Bowl Sunday, we decided to have a party in our room. Emily's choice was Red Lobster take-out, including seafood, steak, and chicken—all her favorites. We phoned in the order and sent a brave Jerry to get it. In spite of our circumstances, we managed to have a great time that night—sort of like a queen and her court—watching football and stuffing our faces. We crowned our party by ordering sundaes from the hotel hospitality shop. We slept so soundly that we were almost late for our clinic appointment!

Arriving on time, however, we were first sent to audiology where Emily had a hearing test, which provided baseline data for comparison after her chemo was begun. More importantly, this test was required when giving chemo for *ovarian* cancer, underlining to us the staff's belief that Emily's cancer was not small bowel.

After the audiological evaluation was completed, we returned to the clinic so Emily's port-a-cath could be accessed. Pat Cobb, the head nurse in the clinic and an incurable optimist, had applied a numbing cream called EMLA to the site on Emily's chest where the port was buried. After about an hour, she removed the cream and inserted the hooked needle through Emily's skin into the port surface. The procedure was generally painless and took only a few minutes to complete.

Once the port was accessed, Emily's blood was drawn. Any IV fluids would go through the port tubing, which could be left in place for as long as seven days before needing to be changed. We quickly realized the value of this type of central line.

By mid-morning, Dr. Dunsmore came to us with the news that Massachusetts General had not yet sent a report. We would have to wait another day.

Janet Stewart, a nurse clinician, met with us to review Emily's blood counts and to teach us the basics of reading the printouts ourselves. Emily's chemo schedule would be determined in part by her blood counts. The more patients and parents knew about blood studies, the easier it was to cope with necessary changes and delays.

Janet showed us that Emily's red-cell count was very low. She said they wanted to transfuse two units of blood on Tuesday before the chemo was begun. Immediately I had thoughts of HIV and other blood-borne diseases. Janet assured us that screening techniques were advanced and the likelihood of Emily contracting a serious disease was minimal. She said we would be amazed at the difference the "new" blood would make in Emily. While nervous about another first-time experience, we agreed to go ahead.

With no other tests required that afternoon, we

Consider it pure joy, my brothers,

whenever you face trials of many kinds,

because you know that the testing of your faith

develops perseverance.

—James 1:2–3

returned to the hotel and relaxed for the remainder of the day. By this time we were adept at playing the waiting game.

Tuesday's clinic appointment started with the transfusion of two units of blood, which took several hours. As Emily sat in the recliner chair, the red droplets slipping silently into her port, an astonishing change occurred before our eyes. Real color returned to her face and energy appeared to tingle in her limbs. Any doubts we might have had about the blood were quickly banished.

During the transfusion, Dr. Dunsmore came into the room and closed the door behind her. Sitting directly across from Jerry and me, she told us that the University of Virginia, St. Jude's, and Massachusetts General all agreed that Emily's cancer was small bowel. She said that Emily was the youngest person *ever* to receive this diagnosis. Emily, who appeared unfazed by the news, confidently stated that she was not afraid. She trusted her doctors. And that was that.

With her childlike innocence, Emily asked Dr. Dunsmore if she would be famous. She seemed pleased when Dr. Dunsmore said her case would likely make medical journals and textbooks. In fact, Dr. Dunsmore and Mark A. Lovell, MD, wrote an article about Emily that was published in the *Journal of Pediatric Hematology/ Oncology* 20(5): 498–501, September/October 1998. That night, however, I wrote in my journal: "I will be overjoyed if the *defeat* of her cancer makes the journals and textbooks."

Dr. Dunsmore quickly recognized that Jerry and I had not handled the diagnosis as well as Emily and invited us to join her in another room. Jerry was overcome by grief and buried his tearful face in my lap as she told us that she did not have a cure for Emily. She quickly followed up this statement by saying that miracles did occur in medicine. Again there was the glimmer of hope. Abraham received his miracle. Maybe Emily-Isaac would receive hers, too.

Wanting to present us with all our options, Dr. Dunsmore explained that she had already been in contact with St. Jude's, which had offered to treat Emily there and to include her in their ongoing study of children with colorectal cancers. Because Emily did not fit the parameters of their study, however, Dr. Dunsmore recommended that we not go. I felt tremendous relief knowing we would not need to make eight-hundred-mile trips to and from Memphis. Instead, we could receive treatment in what had become to us a "local" hospital, near friends, family, and a medical staff we had come to love and trust.

After the transfusion was completed, Emily was sent to nuclear medicine for a bone scan. Through her port, she was injected with a radioactive dye, which took about two hours to spread throughout her skeletal system. While waiting for the dye to disperse, she went back to the CT department, where she began sipping the required three cups of "cocktail" so that chest and abdomen scans could be made. She was allowed to drink clear liquids along with the CT juice, so the three of us went to the hospital cafeteria where Emily "enjoyed" Jell-O, a soft drink, and her juice cocktail. She was pretty miserable.

Because the bone scan used no x-rays, I was allowed to remain in the room with Emily while the scan was completed. An eerie feeling crept over me as I watched an image of my daughter's skull, eye sockets, nose, and teeth appear on the screen. Slowly the loud, humming machine progressed down the length of her body to her feet, until I could see her full skeleton. Emily, who was fascinated with the picture, later requested and received a copy of the image. We have it still.

At the time I did not think about it, but two or three years earlier, Emily had a small part in a local production of *Treasure Island*. Out of the entire acting company, she was the only skeleton. My spirit still shivers ever so slightly when I look at the picture of a smiling skeleton Emily—Treasure Island's only little bag of bones.

In something of a surprise move, Dr. Dunsmore informed us late Tuesday afternoon that St. Jude's had agreed to include Emily in their study after all, while the protocol was delivered at the University of Virginia. This option would offer the best of both worlds, as it were, providing the hospital's Human Investigation Committee (HIC) gave its approval. The start of chemotherapy would be delayed one day while approval was obtained. Denial of the request never occurred to us. A one-day delay was not a problem, either. As I said, we were used to waiting.

After Emily's CT scans were completed, she was sent to the seventh floor to be admitted in preparation for the start of chemo on Wednesday. She received instruction in what would become an important part of her personal hygiene. Mouth care, she was told, would have to be meticulous, with tooth brushing as much as four times daily. Poor mouth care could create an environment ripe for the introduction of infection at a time when, due to low blood counts, Emily's immune system could not ward it off. She quickly realized the seriousness of her role and seemed willing to participate in the strict regimen.

Emily had worn braces for several years and had anticipated their removal within months of her diagnosis. I found myself concerned about the wires and bands in her mouth as I learned more about the harsh side effects of the chemo. When I asked Dr. Dunsmore if the braces should be removed, she preferred to take a wait-and-see approach. Even knowing that it would probably have cost us yet another day's delay while the braces were removed, I wish now I had pushed harder for it to be done. Perhaps Emily could have been spared some of the agony that lay ahead.

By Tuesday night, the stage was set for the most important production of Emily's short life. In the privacy of her room, we rejoiced together about the news that the bone scan was completely clear. No cancer had invaded her skeletal structure. To the surprise of her doctors, it never did. I believe this was one of the miracles Emily received. That night we also rejoiced that the CT scans revealed surgical healing as expected.

I have wondered occasionally if on that winter evening Emily's spirit knew something of the trials that lay ahead of her. At dinner she ate and enjoyed a huge amount of food, including lasagna, salad, milk, a soft drink, macaroni and cheese, *two* Reese's peanut butter cups, *and* a cup of frozen yogurt—with sprinkles—to polish off the meal. Emily would not again eat with such gusto for a very long time.

Not wanting to be alone, she asked me to stay at the hospital with her that night. As he had on many previous nights, Jerry headed to the hotel alone. Wanting more privacy and the option of a "personal" television, weeks earlier Jerry had given up staying at the Ronald McDonald House when he had found out that the cancer insurance would pay for a hotel room. I unfolded the parent chair, unrolled my sleeping bag, and settled in for the night. Emily and I watched television until shortly after midnight. We read some scripture, said prayers, then turned out the lights.

In the dimmed room, I lay still on my "bed." Looking around, I was aware of the IV pump beeping softly while the yellow light at the end of Emily's bed blinked on and off. From the corner of my eye, I glimpsed the small, cut-out paper angels that turned gently in the breezes of the room as they hung silently from an unused IV pole that descended from the ceiling.

"Emily's angels," as we called them, were a gift from a lady whom I had never met. In the weeks before Emily's first hospitalization, I had, on the recommendation of a mutual friend, called Susie to seek advice, since her own daughter had had something of a mysterious illness some months before. I listened as Susie shared her story and encouraged me to be assertive as I desperately sought answers.

Weeks later, when she learned of the seriousness of Emily's illness, she sent me a card with sweet words of encouragement. Inside the card were the folded paper angels. Once pressed open, they could be hung by the thread that had been used to sew them together. They were the representation of the guardian angels assigned by God to protect Emily every day. Countless times during Emily's illness, I read Psalm 91:11–12 aloud to her: "For he will command his angels concerning you to guard you in all your ways; they will lift you up in their hands, so that you will not strike your foot against a stone."

Emily's precious angels hung above her bed at *every* hospitalization. At home they hung above her favorite spot on the couch. Once, we forgot to remove them when she was discharged from the hospital. Panicked, we later returned to find them still hanging above the empty bed, unnoticed by either the cleaning or medical staff.

As Emily's cancer progressed, angels—both seen and unseen—played an ever-more important role in her life until the blessed day when they accompanied her into eternity.

Chapter 6

One of the nurses said it looked like a
lawnmower had gone through my mouth.

—*Girls' Life 1, no. 2:21*
(Oct./Nov. 1994)

Wednesday, February 2, began with little fanfare. Emily ate a light breakfast, then tackled her mouth care. Later that morning, nurse clinician Janet Stewart elaborated on the chemotherapy protocol. Emily's treatment would follow a five-step sequence, beginning and ending with an antinausea pill. Several powerful drugs would be administered by IV over a period of a little more than three hours.

The actual cancer drug was 5-Fluorouracil, called 5-FU for short, along with an enhancing agent called leucovorin. This treatment plan would be repeated on each of five consecutive days, followed by three "off" weeks. Emily was also scheduled to receive injections of an experimental drug that was thought to boost the immune system. She would get these shots three times a week for three consecutive weeks. The fourth week was deemed a "rest" week when Emily's chemically ravaged system could rebuild itself. The cycle could not be repeated until her blood counts had recovered to a level sufficiently high to withstand another treatment series.

According to hospital protocol, Emily would receive her first week of chemotherapy in the hospital. The remaining treatments in the eight-month course could be administered through the out-patient clinic. We were warned that some side effects could cause additional hospitalizations. I took sketchy notes on the abundant information regarding Emily's treatment. Janet reassured me that I would soon understand the process. She also said that everything was ready pending the Human Investigation Committee's approval of the St. Jude study.

After lunch, Emily decided to go to school. The Hospital Education Program (HEP) was a state operated program administered through the Charlottesville City Schools. In fact, for children hospitalized at UVA Children's Medical Center (CMC) and two other hospitals within the state, education services comparable to those provided in regular public schools were mandated in the Code of Virginia. Fortunately for us, Jerry and I knew the program's director, Nancy Artis, having worked with her many years earlier.

From Emily's first day of admission, when Ginger Ellingwood had invited her to participate in the HEP's closed-circuit television program, the HEP teachers had also encouraged her to participate in school and other extracurricular programs offered. The HEP opened the door for her to continue her seventh-grade studies as an enrolled student. Jerry and I were absolutely thrilled that she could go to school, as we believed it offered a perfect distraction from the stresses of hospitalization.

Closed-circuit television shows were broadcast four days a week. *Confetti* became Emily's favorite, but she also participated in *Backstage Virginia*, a program that concentrated on Virginia history; as well as *Wet Paint*, an art show; and *CMC Live*, a show featuring the CMC's beloved mascot bear, Charles Major Claus, or "Charley" for short. The live broadcasts were geared to different age groups and encouraged children to develop their sense of creativity, identity, and belonging during their hospital stays. Emily occasionally went to the seventh floor studio to participate "live." More often, however, she preferred to participate through her bed phone.

Emily quickly endeared herself to many of the HEP staff. It would be safe to say, however, that she was most attached to Marta Gilliam, the teacher assigned to the adolescent-age group. From their first meeting, student and teacher shared a special bond. Marta could read Emily well, knowing when to encourage and when to retreat. Emily often armored herself with Marta's words, especially when my teacher-self tried to push her too hard.

"Mother," Emily would assert, "Marta said I'm good at this stuff, and I don't need to do all the problems." Back-off time for teacher Mom.

Indeed, as a longtime special education teacher myself, I knew the value of finding alternate ways to cover material. Acknowledging that this was necessary for my own child was difficult. Despite my reservations, under Marta's tutelage, Emily continued to make excellent academic progress. Beyond academics, however, it was Marta who inspired Emily to explore her feelings and to express herself with a bold creativeness. It was Marta who put the world at Emily's fingertips.

Late Wednesday afternoon, Dr. Dunsmore delivered the wonderful news that the HIC had approved Emily's participation in the St. Jude study. She added that the board *never* agreed to such things but would do it for Emily. Could this change of heart have been another little miracle? Yes. And without further delay, Emily's chemotherapy was begun. She watched intently as the IV lines were changed and the leucovorin was started. She continued her observations throughout the entire process, including the administration of 5-FU and antinausea medications. By ten o'clock, the first round was completed, and she'd suffered no ill effects.

Dr. McGahren stopped by Emily's room to tell her that earlier in the day, her case had been discussed by the Tumor Board. This group of doctors had devoted an hour of their discussion to her cancer. Emily was impressed with Dr. McGahren's report that she had "turned the medical world upside down."

> "For I know the plans I have for you," declares the Lord,
>
> "plans to prosper you and not to harm you,
>
> plans to give you hope and a future."
>
> —*Jeremiah 29:11*

Before Emily went to sleep that night, she asked me serious and difficult questions. "How widespread is my cancer? What if the diagnosis is wrong? Am I dying?"

Answering the first two questions was relatively easy. The third question wrenched my heart and my spirit. "Emily," I said, "you're not dying. But why don't you ask Dr. Dunsmore tomorrow. You'll feel better hearing it from her."

The next morning she did ask Dr. Dunsmore, whose response was the same as my own. Emily, who had absolute confidence in Dr. Dunsmore, was content.

Emily awoke Thursday morning feeling very well. She ate breakfast, completed her mouth care, and headed for school. The chemotherapy was started at one o'clock. Just as she had done during the first treatment, she watched closely as a resident administered the drugs. Suddenly, she sat bolt upright in bed and announced in a panic-ridden voice that the resident was "doing it wrong." A nurse was called immediately, and she verified Emily's observation. No harm was done, and the process was completed correctly. Had Emily not been her own watchdog, the error would have gone unnoticed, at least at that point.

A short while after the chemotherapy was completed that day, Emily received her first injection of the drug that the doctors hoped would boost her immune system, and by late that night, she began to experience the first side effects. Her head throbbed, including her teeth and jaw. The pain was visible in her eyes and in her constant movement. Neither Tylenol nor my massaging fingers brought her relief. Silently I prayed for Emily, begging God to heal her and to give me the strength to watch her suffer. I clung to the scripture from Mark 11:24 that says that whatever we ask for, if we believe that we have received it, it will be ours. How I longed for the manifestation of that promise!

Emily slept little that night. Shortly after eight on Friday morning, she fell into an exhausted sleep. While she slept, pediatric oncologist Dr. De Alarcon told me that medicines were available to help control the side effects. He encouraged me to call him or any member of the cancer team at any hour. He ordered codeine, which relieved her headache for a short while.

Within minutes of the administration of 5-FU on the third day, Emily suffered another violent headache from which she did not get relief until Dr. De Alarcon ordered morphine. He suspected that she was in the small group of people who could not tolerate the particular antinausea drug that they had prescribed for her. Acting on his suspicion, he ordered a different medication, which made Emily very sleepy but was a welcomed alternative to her headaches. The third immune booster injection was also given.

By nighttime, she had a temperature and other flulike symptoms. She felt so bad that she refused to do her mouth care. Jerry and I sensed the drawing of battle lines. Although we hated to do it, we firmly insisted that she complete at least a minimum amount of mouth care.

By the fourth day of chemo, the headaches were better controlled. We soon realized that constipation would be a significant problem, however. She ate and drank very little. Most fluid intake was through the IV. Combined with the constipating effects of the pain medications, she soon experienced severe bowel discomfort.

Sunday, February 6, marked the fifth and final day of Emily's first week of chemotherapy. According to the protocol, it was the day on which she should have been discharged. She had become so constipated, however, that her trips to the bathroom resulted in screams of pain. Three times she nearly fainted, yelling that everything was turning black as she grabbed for the restroom wall. Emily was checked thoroughly by the residents, who ordered a bag of IV fluid to be pushed over a three-hour period. Their plan worked, and she experienced no more near-fainting episodes. Medications were ordered to ease the constipation. She would not go home on this day.

The quiet of Sunday afternoon was broken when a surgical resident entered Emily's room and somewhat abruptly announced that he was going to remove the stitches that remained from her second operation. He told Emily that Dr. McGahren had used a type of running stitch that could be removed easily by snipping the exposed thread at the top, middle, and bottom of her incision. All that was necessary was to clip the thread and pull out the suture material. Simple. The procedure would take no more than two or three minutes.

Emily was far from convinced by this doctor's words. As he stood poised over her bed, scissors and tweezers in hand, she flatly refused every approach this poor young surgeon made toward her abdomen. I watched, stunned, as he lost his battle with her. With unmistakable exasperation in his voice, the doctor told Emily the stitches could not be left in her belly permanently. Sooner or later she would have to submit.

"I'll do it tomorrow," she announced with conviction.

Silently conceding his loss, the doctor left the room. I did not know whether to laugh or cry. Emily looked at me for reassurance. Fire still burned in her eyes.

"They're going to have to do it soon," I said gently.

"Not today, Momma. I just can't do it today," Emily sighed.

In my heart, I knew she had been robbed of the right to make many decisions. I did not blame her for asserting herself wherever possible. In my head, I knew that procrastinating on the removal of the sutures would only bring more stress for her when she could no longer negotiate a delay.

On Monday morning, Emily's IV was stopped and her port was de-accessed. Though she screamed with pain, she finally had a bowel movement. In general she seemed better. In the early afternoon, a different surgical resident came to remove her stitches. Not surprisingly, she would not permit this man anywhere near her. I shook my head in amazement at her successful foil of the surgical team's second attempt to remove her sutures. Fortunately, one of my favorite seventh floor pediatric residents came to the rescue. Emily was fond of this doctor, too, and agreed to let him remove the stitches.

The fight wasn't over, however. This poor man quickly found himself lured onto Emily's battlefield. He never retreated and firmly told her he was going to proceed. He instructed me to hold Emily's hands above her head, which I did. Huge tears tumbled from her eyes as he gently gripped one end of the blue thread with his tweezers and pulled. In theory, the running stitch should have slipped out with minimal resistance. In reality, her skin was lifted into a sharp peak four or five inches high as the doctor pulled with more force. The resistance was so great that the sutures were removed in pieces. The last piece broke off at the skin level, where it remained.

"It's over, Emily," the resident said with compassion.

I wiped away her tears and handed her a tissue. Too drained to speak, she said nothing.

Late that afternoon, Emily said her throat felt sore. She had no fever, however, and an infection was not suspected. We were told she was ready for discharge. Against Emily's wishes, Jerry and I loaded the van, and the three of us headed for home.

By early evening, her throat was worse. Her face, cheeks, and lips began to swell. She would not take even small sips of a chocolate milkshake, which had long been a favorite comfort food. She was unable to open her mouth enough to take any medication. She slept in short naps, waking hourly with soft whimpers and groans.

The following morning Emily had a scheduled appointment at the Primary Care Center (PCC), an outpatient facility adjacent to University Hospital. Before leaving for Charlottesville, she tried to brush her teeth and use her mouthwash, but her mouth was too swollen and painful to do either. I could see dime-sized white blisters on the inside of her lips. She uttered no words, just soft sounds in response to our *yes* or *no* questions. I put a glob of EMLA over her port and covered it with clear adhesive so her skin would be numb by the time we arrived at the clinic. I hoped an IV pain medication would be started as soon as possible.

The clinic was packed with noisy, anxious children. We signed in and took our seats among the many families waiting to be seen. Emily, who was unable to hold up her head, rested against Jerry's arm.

Pat Cobb, the head nurse whose care of cancer kids is legendary in the clinic, happened to walk by and see Emily, her face swollen and full of pain. Pat immediately took her into a vacant examination room and within a few minutes started an IV morphine drip. Before long, Dr. Dunsmore told us Emily would need to be admitted for treatment of her ulcers. Poor Emily just looked at us with relief. She knew she should never have gone home. In that regard, she was never wrong, but in the early months of her treatment, neither her parents nor doctors knew to listen. In time we would.

By the time Emily was in a room, it was the middle of the afternoon. Eating was impossible due to the raw ulcers that dotted the inside of her mouth. Her braces, of which she had once been so proud, now aggravated the sores further. She could not even move her tongue to form words. Swallowing was difficult. The IV kept her hydrated, but morphine offered the best relief. That day I learned how 5-FU works: it attacks the alimentary canal, which technically begins at the lips and extends the full path that food follows through the body—right to its elimination point. That meant that ulcers were almost certainly present from Emily's beginning to her end. For the next eight days, she did little more than exist in her hospital room. Even with morphine, her suffering was heart-wrenching.

Thankfully, Dr. Dunsmore recommended that Emily's braces be removed as soon as possible. An appointment was made with the PCC Dental Clinic for the following week. Emily would never again see her orthodontist. Nor would she achieve the hoped-for "perfect" smile. She didn't care. She was completely happy with the one she had.

Emily's discharge was scheduled for February 16, one day ahead of my forty-fourth birthday. Before we could leave, however, she had an appointment with Lynn Woodson, who was editor of *CMC Pinwheel,* a hospital publication featuring "news from around the Children's Medical Center." Lynn wanted to write an article about a school-age patient, and Emily had been recommended to her. I was invited along since Emily's mouth was still painful and talking was hard. In fact, I ended up answering most of Lynn's questions.

We met in the Adolescent Lounge, which was one of Emily's favorite hospital hangouts. The Adolescent—or teen—Lounge was off limits to anyone but staff and teens (teens were given a special code to unlock the door). It was painted black and had a bumper pool table; some comfy, checkered-flag racing-car chairs; and a private, carpet-lined phone booth. Emily loved the lounge and its status, but she was especially enamored of the private phone booth.

Emily did her best to talk to Lynn, but it was clearly painful. Yet Lynn would write, "She faces the future with confidence and looks forward to going home soon." And that summed it up. Emily did look forward to going home soon. Most of all, she wanted to eat! Emily's only quote: "I can't wait to eat Chinese food again."

A picture of Emily is embedded in the article that appeared in the Spring 1994 issue of CMC *Pinwheel*. She is unsmiling; her hair is pulled back in a twisty tie, and her hands rest atop her school books. I think she looks sad in this picture. The truth is, though, the corners of her mouth were just too sore for her to crack a smile.

Lynn would maintain her friendship with Emily throughout the course of her illness. It was Lynn who encouraged Emily to speak through the lens of a camera. Lynn, too, would speak, not through a camera but through carefully penned words describing the inevitable sadness of a flower whose wilting comes much too soon. "Unnatural Alloys" appears on pages 254–255 of this book.

After the interview, Emily and I headed back to her room to finish packing while we waited for the discharge papers. After thirty-five days in the hospital (except for the two short furloughs), going home hardly seemed real. We were excited but afraid at the same time. The discharge papers arrived, and I signed off on them. We made one final check to see that the room was empty, sort of like Jerry does when we check out of a hotel.

We did leave one item behind—a Valentine's poem that Emily had written for the nurses on the seventh floor. She had worked and worked on her poem, asking me for rhyming words here and there. Once it was finished, she had me print it in hot-pink ink, then she adorned the edges with nine ballet stickers (pointe shoes). She signed the bottom, "Love, Emily Jones." She presented it to one of the nurses on Valentine's Day. It was pinned on the nurses' station bulletin board and remained there for months. Here is her untitled poem:

As Valentine's Day approaches this year,
Seven Central gets ready to bring forth some cheer
To kids who are bound by tubes and by pumps
To a life on their backs, their sides, or their rumps.

It's 3 a.m. and in sneaks a nurse,
"I've got some medicine so you won't get worse.
This won't hurt, sweetie. I'll be just a minute!
Go back to sleep now. Your gown? Sure, I'll pin it!"

So time marches on to seven o'clock rounds:
"Are you eating? Are you drinking? Have you gained
*   any pounds?"*
"Ah, let me see here . . . You've some stitches to come
*   out?*
Now, this won't hurt, Emily! What are you crying
*   about?"*

With a nurse at my side and mom at my head,
The doc isn't so scary bending over my bed.
With scissors and tweezers secure in his hand,
My patience and stillness he's sure to demand.

"There now, all done. That wasn't so bad.
It's time to cheer up. Stop looking so sad."
And so with encouragement, faith, and good skill,
A few IV's, a shot, or a tiny red pill,

The nurses and doctors good care of me take,
Until to home quick tracks I can make.
So thank you I say on [this] Valentine's Day.
You make my life comfortable while in Hotel U.VA.

Heading west, we crested Afton Mountain in a brilliant, late afternoon sun. Eyes suddenly brimming with tears, Emily looked at me and whispered, "I didn't think I'd ever get home." Tears rolled shamelessly out of my eyes as I silently reached over and grabbed her thin, pale hand. How many times had I had the exact same thought?

Emily returned to school the next day. She was something of a celebrity. I like to think of the gaggle of girls gathered around her as she walked between classes, giving them the lowdown on cute residents, her favorite nurses, the surgeries, and school in the hospital. She was fully and vibrantly alive, appreciating like few others how good it was to be just another seventh grader in middle school. By her return home that afternoon, she had homework and typical teenage stories to share at the dinner table. Most of all, she had plans for her future.

Her most immediate plan was to celebrate her thirteenth birthday, now just a few days away. Her illness, surgeries, and long hospitalization had consumed so much of my physical and emotional energy that I had to turn some of the planning over to Jerry, who rented a local indoor miniature golf course for Emily's party.

"Happy Birthday Emily" greeted us on the outside marquee that Saturday afternoon as we pulled into the parking lot. Many of Emily's friends and family were present, including her grandparents; her cousin Shannon and her aunt Carol; my sister, Ann; and Ann's dear friend and housemate, Lynn. Emily and her friends played miniature golf, laughed, talked, and celebrated in a most wonderful, normal way. Emily blew out the thirteen candles atop her cake, which was decorated with a ballerina in a pink tutu.

Of course, I worried about the risk of infection, since her blood counts were most likely low due to the chemotherapy, but the danger of infection was offset that day by the smile on Emily's face and her delight in hanging out with friends while she celebrated becoming a bona fide teenager.

Chapter 7

I did my best,
and that's all that counts.

—Emily's diary,
June 1, 1994

A few days after her birthday, Emily started her second round of chemotherapy at the PCC. As usual, I put EMLA over her port before we left home. The trip to Charlottesville felt as normal as going on a shopping trip. Her mouth was completely healed, and she seemed strong and ready for the second round. She hopped off the elevator on the fourth floor and greeted the clinic nurses as if they were old buddies.

She was assigned a clinic room, then settled herself into the big vinyl chair. I watched as Pat Cobb expertly plunged in the hooked needle. Emily flinched a bit but said it didn't really hurt. It hurt me to watch. Blood was drawn, and a short while later we got the go-ahead to start the chemo. Like so many cancer families, we were beginning to strike a manageable treatment rhythm.

I accompanied Emily to the clinic every day that week, but over the months to follow we developed a system that allowed *me* to get in some work hours and *her* to have a little freedom. On clinic days, she and I headed to Charlottesville early in the morning. I dropped her off at the street level, and she went alone to the fourth floor.

Looking back, I wonder about the safety of that plan. At the time, I thought nothing of it. She exited the car, waved good-bye, and marched into the crowd of professionals and patients coming and going from the PCC. Emily loved it. She spent the day at the clinic, and I spent time at my job. Jerry drove to Charlottesville after his school let out to pick her up.

Emily's chemotherapy took several hours to administer but not all day. Sometimes she just chilled, watched television, or talked to the PCC staff. So far as we know, she never caused a problem. Actually, I remember one of the clinic nurses telling me that they often found little odd jobs for Emily to do. I know she delighted in that sort of responsibility.

As an educational consultant, Ginger Ellingwood was assigned to two clinics: Hematology/Oncology (HEM/ONC) and Renal. Because Emily was a cancer patient, she was followed through HEM/ONC.

Ginger's work was full of challenges. Most hematology (blood disorder) patients are chronically ill and are followed in clinic for many years. By contrast, cancer patients are acutely ill and are typically followed for a relatively shorter time. Regardless, to be effective Ginger had to balance a good listening ear against the need to help patients sort through the reality and limitations of their diseases.

As warranted, educational consultants made on-site visits to their students' schools. These visits provided school personnel and classmates an opportunity for give-and-take discussions about the chronic conditions or serious illnesses of school-age patients. Ginger scheduled a spring visit to Emily's school.

Lessons from Emily

Years later, Ginger shared that this school visit was set apart for her simply by the fact that Emily wanted to "do all the talking." Ginger was a self-described "highly structured teacher," and she wondered how Emily's solo plan would fly, particularly with the tough middle-school population. But then she thought, "This is Emily we're talking about!"

Emily never had an "Oh, woe is me" attitude about her cancer. Instead, she believed, "If I can get this cancer, so can you!" And she wanted everybody to know it. I don't think she was out to frighten people; she just believed lightning could strike anywhere, anytime—as it had done in her own life.

The morning of Ginger's visit arrived. Emily left home excited and not a bit nervous, mainly because she was not speaking to the entire student body but only to members of her seventh-grade team, which might have been as many as 150 people. During one of the morning class blocks, students and teachers filed into the school's forum. Ginger still remembers the faces of the students who sat in the front row. As the group grew larger and more daunting, she sensed a bit of hesitation from Emily. All they needed to do was look at each other and a silent agreement was reached that the presentation would be a team effort.

Ginger wisely suggested that Emily start by introducing the name of her cancer. That nudge was all it took to jumpstart Emily. The rest of her talk just flowed. Ginger wrote of her, "She accomplished what she set out to do." Later that day, when Jerry asked Emily how her talk had gone, she simply said, "I wish I'd had more time to talk."

I wish I could have been a fly on the forum wall that day. I would have liked to hear Emily's description of her cancer in her own words. Just as much as she wanted her classmates to know that they, too, could get cancer, she also wanted them to understand that she was still an ordinary teenager with hopes and dreams like everyone else.

Like Marta, Ginger became a pillar in Emily's life. But Emily left her own mark on their lives, too. Ginger would write to me many years later:

> Once Emily began treatment, I remained in awe of her spirit to keep going even when it got really rough . . . her willingness to continue with school as much as she could, even though she saw lots of folks staring because of the change in appearance, her desire to meet academic expectations when I know her teachers would have been so willing to be flexible. At no time did Emily ever ask for or expect anything different at school.

To Emily, cancer was more of a nuisance than any sort of limitation. It got in her way, especially with her dancing. Later in 1994, she was asked to help the younger dancers prepare for that year's production of *The Nutcracker*, but her surgeries and treatments meant that she could neither continue her lessons nor perform. In fact, I don't believe she again put on her pointe shoes following the 1993 performance. She simply pushed her well-worn dance bag into a corner of her bedroom closet and forgot about it.

I found it months after she passed away. I sat on her daybed and held it on my lap for a long time, trying to decide whether or not to open it. The urge to see the contents was overwhelming, however, and I slowly unzipped the soiled pink bag. There, staring me in the face, were her pointe shoes with the ribbons tightly wrapped around them. The toes were still stuffed with cotton. Her pink tights were crumpled just the way she had left them, with her pink leotard and matching skirt underneath. No one had disturbed them since she'd last touched them.

I have much to write to you, but I do not want to do so with pen and ink.

I hope to see you soon, and we will talk face to face.

—3 John 1:13–14

Afraid to breathe, I curled my fingers around the shoes and gently lifted them from their tomb, clutching them against my chest. Oh, sweet Lord. Emily glided across the stage in these shoes, her green party dress swishing and her ringlet curls bobbing to the music. She seemed so incredibly happy then.

I cried a lot that afternoon, not stopping until the thought came to me that Emily now dances with angels. Only then did my tears cease.

Seven days after Emily finished her second round of chemo, she was admitted to the hospital with ulcers. Again, morphine helped. It was during this admission, however, that we thought she might be getting a little too much morphine. The signs were clear in her uncharacteristic crankiness. She demanded that the room be kept as dark as possible. No one could talk. The chair had to form a perfect triangle against the window ledge. Personal items on the windowsill had to be maintained in perfect order. She got so upset with the ticking clock that we had to unplug and remove it from the wall.

Bubbles, as well as Emily's paternal grandparents (Elmer and Ocie, whom she called PawPaw and MeeMaw), got their feelings hurt over some unkind comments. In truth, all of us were stung at one time or another. Finally, Jerry had had enough and complained to the nursing staff. I remember her nurse saying that it didn't matter how cranky Emily became, they were there to help her feel better. Well, the morphine dose *was* reduced, and we *all* felt better—including Emily.

By St. Patrick's Day, Emily was feeling substantially improved and was hopeful that she would be discharged soon. Rather on the spur of the moment, she decided it would be fun to throw a "green party" for the doctors and nurses who worked on 7 Central. Her party would be held in the Adolescent Lounge.

Marta and Flo, the teaching assistant, worked double time rounding up the must-have materials. Emily made green cookies and sliced green vegetables. She made green dip and some sort of green drink. She had green cups and napkins. She also made a green mess. As luck would have it, she also got discharged on the same afternoon as her party.

In my excitement to leave, I completely forgot about the green refreshments that were spread across the table in the Adolescent Lounge. A pair of green angels must have cleaned up everything. I remain grateful to Marta and Flo for doing a little magic on Emily's behalf. She left the hospital that afternoon as happy as any leprechaun in Ireland.

Chapter 8

Even though I have no hair,
I know this treatment is very fair.

—excerpt from poem
written by Emily,
May 1994

Blessings came to us in unexpected ways throughout Emily's cancer journey. One afternoon several months into her treatment, I received a call from my good friend Betsy Curry. Betsy and I had met when our first-born children were infants sharing the same babysitter. Both of our second children were named Emily. Our Emily was a little more than a year older than Betsy's.

Over the years, we went on many happy outings with our children. One of the most memorable was the day in December 1985 when we took all four children to the theater to see the animated cartoon, *101 Dalmatians*. Three-year-old Emily Curry had become totally absorbed in the movie, but neither Betsy nor I realized just how absorbed until a pack of yapping dogs raced across the screen in an effort to rescue puppies from the clutches of Cruella De Vil.

Without warning, Emily C. stood up and began barking loudly. She put her little hands on the seat in front of her and leaped over it in one movement, still barking at full capacity. Every head turned in her direction, but she was completely oblivious. Betsy and I howled with laughter. We still laugh about it today.

On this particular day, however, Betsy hadn't called to reminisce about the past. She'd called to tell me of a dream she'd had several nights earlier. In her dream, she was peering down on the Earth. Moonbeams arched forth from around the globe. Countless prayers were rising to heaven on the moonbeams, and each was for my Emily. Even now I can envision the blue Earth with innumerable silvery beams directing thousands—hundreds of thousands—of prayers to the Creator's throne.

Over time, this dream would prove to be prophetic, as prayer warriors around the globe rallied on Emily's behalf. I am convinced that not one of those prayers slipped by God unnoticed or unanswered according to His infinite wisdom and grace.

Two of the most powerful prayer warriors were Karen, a teaching colleague at my school, and Sharon, her identical twin sister. Karen's walk with the Lord was (and is) faith-filled and bold. Her sister was a carbon copy in every way, including her faith. Sometime in the early months of Emily's illness, Karen and Sharon began sending us letters that were full of scripture references and words of encouragement. Sometimes the "voice" of their letters came directly from the Lord; other times not. I read the letters over and over, often aloud to Emily. None of them were dated; they just arrived when the Lord knew we most needed a word of encouragement.

One day a letter appeared on my desk at school. "Gird Up" was printed in neat lettering on the front of the envelope. In the same neat print, on the back was written, "Our job is to stand on His Word; it's His job to perform it." I opened it to find eight pages of handwritten encouragement:

> You cannot out-trust God! God picks the timing. In Ecclesiastes 3, it says: "To everything there is a season and a time to

every purpose under heaven: a time to die; a time to plant and a time to pluck up that which is planted; a time to kill and a time to *heal*; a time to break down and a time to build up." . . . I don't write this saying to prepare for death—there is time for that after the fact. Now is the time to build up—stand on his Word! Show God a faith in his Word that does not waver or fall. We might think that God is late—but he's not. God is always right on time.

Much of the remainder of the letter followed the same vein: *do not trust in the natural world; trust God, and wait. He is always on time.* How many times had I reminded myself of this spiritual truth? I'd believed it for many years and had seen evidence of it in my own life. But when my daughter's life hung in the balance, it was difficult to overlook the natural world and wait on God's perfect timing. I prayed for Emily's healing over and over. Natural time was not on her side, and I wanted an immediate miracle.

In the end, it would be the words of the Apostle Paul in Romans 8:38–39 that would bring me peace, promise, and confidence: "For I am convinced that neither death nor life, neither angels nor demons, neither the present nor the future, nor any powers, neither height nor depth, nor anything else in all creation, will be able to separate us from the love of God that is in Christ Jesus our Lord."

Those words assured me that nothing could come between Emily and the love of God. Not even death. That's all that really mattered. Yes, it is utterly important to trust in the Lord and wait for his timing, which is perfect. No matter what happens to us *in the natural world,* we cannot be separated from the love of God. Peace flooded over me when this scripture engraved itself on my heart. It unlocked the secret of confident waiting on the Lord.

Scripture verses for Emily were also included in Karen's "gird up" letter: "Before I formed you in the womb I knew you, before you were born I set you apart; I appointed you as a prophet to the nations" (Jeremiah 1:5) and "'for I am with you and will rescue you,' declares the Lord" (Jeremiah 1:8). These words both comforted and strengthened Emily. She asked me to read the verses aloud many times. Two months before she died, the Lord would speak them to her again in a profound and dramatic fashion.

Still other blessings flowed down upon us. The cancer insurance policy that Jerry had taken out in May 1993 provided cash to cover missed days from work after our sick leave was depleted (I ran out of sick days within the first month of Emily's illness). Often a card would arrive with "just a little something" to help us out tucked inside. Not until I wrote this book did I learn that these gifts totaled more than $8,000 over the course of Emily's illness. By the grace of God and through the loving kindness of our friends and family, we lacked for nothing. Although we missed an enormous amount of time from work, every bill was paid.

> The Lord is good, a refuge in times of trouble.
>
> He cares for those who trust in him.
>
> *—Nahum 1:7*

Jerry was meticulous about recording the amount of monetary gifts on the inside of the cards so that I could write notes of thanks. Then one day, a business envelope arrived in the mail. It had no return address. Inside I found a white, dispenser-type paper towel. Written in large block lettering was this message: GAS AND/OR WHATEVER GOD BLESS YOU. Every few weeks, another envelope arrived with a similar paper towel message. Each envelope contained at least $20. In all, our paper-towel friend, whose identity remains a mystery, sent more than $300 *for gas and/or whatever*. God bless this kind friend.

Amazingly, or perhaps by design, Emily's treatment schedule allowed her to be at home for most major holidays. She finished her third round of chemo on Good Friday. Easter Sunday saw all five of us dressed in our Easter best and worshipping in church together.

To make that holy day even more special, Emily was confirmed during the service. She was, of course, dealing with mouth ulcers, but she still sang—albeit softly—right along with us and the whole congregation. Singing resurrection hymns never felt so good.

Monday morning, Emily was back at school. Report cards came out that week, but she had not completed enough assignments to earn grades. She wasn't concerned. Her teachers were both lenient and gracious in allowing her to complete missed work. To Emily's credit, she did not take advantage of her situation and did her best to submit assignments within a reasonable amount of time. (She did eventually get her report card.) That week after Easter she had just one clinic appointment, so our lives felt amazingly normal.

Emily was happy and upbeat. Jerry and I even managed a date night on Saturday. Remembering the joy of celebrating Easter Sunday as a family at our church, I wrote in my journal at week's end, "Emily's faith is unshakable and she often sustains us." She wrote in her diary that she just wanted to eat.

Within about six weeks of Emily's first chemo, we began to notice long strands of hair on her pillowcase each morning. We'd pick them off one day and more would be in their place the next. We were, of course, expecting her hair to fall out, but the shock of seeing it happen was no less intense. Emily would brush her hair, and I'd pull out the bundles caught in the bristles. Her eyelashes and brows were also falling out.

In a picture taken of her in early spring 1994, the effects of chemo were evident: she was skinny, pale, and her hair was unnaturally thin. Nonetheless, she sported her spunky smile, and her eyes were full of their characteristic twinkle. She was a very sick girl, but she never let it show.

Early in May, she had another hospitalization for side effects of chemo. This one lasted only a few days. Emily knew what to expect and, for the first time, began to insert her own form of control and humor into her hospital life. She started by crafting a set of "info" signs that she posted in plain view on her hospital door. "Do not disturb. I'm getting dressed." "I am at school. Come and get me!" "Do not disturb. I'm busy. Thanks!" "Please do not disturb. I'm sleeping." "Sure come on in. I'm not busy, but are you? See you inside. From the person inside."

Nurses, visitors, and perhaps a few residents and doctors read them and chuckled. Maybe even a few people heeded them, but they did give Emily a bit of autonomy. One day, I returned to her room having run an errand and was met with a message written in red ink on a paper towel: "Mom, gone to X-ray." I found it refreshing and a source of pride that my child was confident and mature beyond her thirteen years. She needed me, but she didn't need me. It made living with her illness much easier.

Later in the month, we were back in the clinic for the fifth round of chemo. After she completed it, her port was de-accessed, and Jerry brought her home. That night she attended a party at a girlfriend's house. I picked her up around ten o'clock and tried my best to get details on the ride home. Not unexpectedly, Emily said little except that she'd had a good time.

Years later, I discovered her account of the event in her diary. The entry was classic Emily. She cut to the chase in her usual way: "It [Ashley's party] was really cool. I didn't dance. We played spin the bottle. I was supposed to kiss someone but I didn't want to." I remain overjoyed that after a week's round of chemo, she had the stamina to attend a party. It had everything to do with her relentless desire to be normal and to make cancer nothing more than an afterthought in her life.

Do I wish I knew the identity of the boy Emily was supposed to kiss? Of course, I do! You would, too. What breaks my heart is the reality that, so far as I know, that refused kiss was her one and only opportunity.

By late May, Emily's hair was coming out in fistfuls. The day after Ashley's party, Emily wrote in her diary: "Today I got my mouth ulcers and boy do they hurt. I pulled out most of my hair. Momma cut off the rest." Watching Emily pull large clumps of hair from her head made my stomach queasy. Worse was taking a large pair of scissors and cutting off the remainder of her wonderful hair. I stuffed all that I could into a Ziploc bag. I still have it stored in a container in the attic. Like a fine perfume, I think of it as *Essence of Emily.*

With baldness came the need to wear the wig that was purchased months earlier. "Cindy" looked amazingly like Emily's own hair, although her real hair had a more reddish tint to it. Not long after she started wearing Cindy, she purchased a floppy denim hat to wear over it. A denim rosebud held up the brim so it would not cover her eyes. She looked cute and hip in her wig and hat. They definitely gave her confidence in the early days of her baldness.

Almost as soon as Emily became ill, friends and family sent lapel pins to her. Mostly they were angels and crosses, but sometimes they represented places or events. For example, she received a Penn State pin, a "World-famous San Diego Zoo" pin, an Idaho potato pin, and a USA Olympic pin. As her collection grew, she had no place to display them until one day when she got the idea of attaching them to her denim hat. The hat quickly became known as the "Pin Hat," and she wore it every time she and Cindy were out in public. It was quite a conversation piece.

Church members were especially eager to add pins to her collection. One member brought pins from her travels to Russia. Other travelers delivered pins from London and Paris and Greece. She also decided to attach her acolyte (candle lighter) pin that read "REBORN IN CHRIST." In all, she put more than eighty-five pins on her denim hat. Today Cindy and the Pin Hat rest atop a manikin head on the dresser in our guest bedroom, not too far from the bookcase that holds her pink ballet shoes with their tightly wrapped ribbons and cotton still stuffed in the toes.

Of the eighty-five pins on Pin Hat, there are more that represent Make-A-Wish than anything else. Theresa Andrews, the social worker on Emily's medical team, was the first person to mention this organization, which would become a huge blessing in our lives. Theresa had been present the day we were given Emily's official diagnosis, and we were blessed that she remained connected throughout the duration of Emily's illness. She often spent time with Emily during clinic visits when Jerry and I were at work. Theresa watched movies with her and took her shopping or on walks. She was a dynamic presence in our daughter's life.

It was in early June that Theresa first spoke to us about becoming involved with Make-A-Wish. Because Emily had a life-threatening illness, she was eligible. Dr. Dunsmore had been consistently adamant that we not procrastinate on any family plans. She encouraged us to plan a Make-A-Wish trip for late summer.

Emily was thrilled with the idea. So Theresa arranged for a wish coordinator from Make-A-Wish to meet with us. He was soft spoken and directed much of his conversation to Emily. It didn't take her long to identify her wish as a trip to the Walt Disney World Resort. The paperwork was completed, and Emily's wish was scheduled to come true in August during her "free" week between the seventh and eighth (final) chemo treatments.

If mouth ulcers had not been a persistent side effect of Emily's treatment, she would have had far fewer hospitalizations. It just so happened that in early June, she was hospitalized again for mouth ulcers. This admission, however, also coincided with the 1994 Children's Miracle Network Telethon. The telethons were part of the national campaign that raised millions of dollars for local children's hospitals across the United States, and the Charlottesville area was noted for donating more money per capita than any other locality in the country.

Several days before the telethon, the Madge M. Jones Activity Terrace, which was a huge play space located on the seventh floor of University Hospital, was converted into a television studio for the two-day event. Miles of electrical cables stretched through the halls of the hospital. A phone bank was set up on the terrace, along with local maps and other telethon props. Rows of chairs were set up for audience participation.

Patients who were well enough were often invited to make cameo appearances on the telethon. It was Marta who first approached Emily about sharing the fish quilt that she had recently designed as part of the HEP's Adolescent Quilting Project. Emily had pieced together a varied background, then appliquéd on six or seven fish, each with crystal air bubbles escaping from its mouth. Local quilters from the Charlottesville Quilters Guild finished it so that it looked very professional.

Emily was delighted to talk about it and the Adolescent Quilting Project during the telethon broadcast. She also wanted to read her Valentine's poem. The night before the telethon she wrote in her diary: "Oh I can't wait till tomorrow. I'm so excited I'm going to be on T.V. I'm a star."

The emcees for the weekend were from the local NBC television station. Fun and fanfare ruled as familiar personalities raised hundreds of thousands of dollars for the Children's Medical Center. One of the most beloved emcees was Robert Van Winkle, the station's popular weatherman. His natural love for children and his television charisma made him a perfect host at the event. He often interviewed the children who came on the air.

Emily's first appearance was truly a cameo as she stood with a group of patients who were featured in the opening minutes of the telethon. She wore a dress and Cindy, but instead of Pin Hat, she wore a very attractive black velvet hat. Her freckles were surprisingly visible on camera. At 10:50 p.m., she made a second appearance, this time with two other patients. Prompted by Robert's questions, Emily explained about her fish quilt. She was completely at ease in front of the camera.

The next afternoon, Emily had a "personal" interview with Robert Van Winkle on camera. The telethon was widely watched within the Charlottesville viewing area, and I had to wonder how many people listened a little closer as Emily, smartly dressed in a sleeveless blouse, along with Cindy Wig and Pin Hat, unhesitatingly answered Robert's questions. Quite matter-of-factly, she stated that she had adenocarcinoma of the small bowel. She quickly followed that statement by saying she was the only child who had ever been diagnosed with that disease.

"Is that so?" Robert asked with true surprise in his voice. Robert closed the interview by asking Emily if she had a poem that she wanted to share with the audience. Sweet Robert wrapped his arm around her as she read her Valentine's poem. He planted a little kiss on her head when she was done.

Emily had made a total of four appearances on the telethon by its close on Sunday evening. Someone snapped a picture of her during her personal interview with Robert. Not long after, we received a copy signed on the back by Robert: "To Emily—A very special young lady—Thanks for your poem—Robert Van Winkle." It is a beautiful, happy picture—to this day one of our favorites.

Emily was discharged on June 7 and was back at school the next day, where she enjoyed notoriety as a result of her television appearances. School would not dismiss for another nine days, so she had time to catch up on missed work and enjoy the last days of seventh grade with her middle-school friends. She had missed so much time that she had actually forgotten her locker number. She later penned in her diary, "That made a lot of people's day!"

The following week, she had yet another CT and bone scan but rejoined her classmates in time for the last day of the school year. She was thrilled to receive two achievement certificates at the closing assembly. Shortly after eating lunch, though, she began to feel ill, and by that night, she was back in the hospital with a suspected intestinal blockage.

She and I were especially sad because our church's Youth Sunday was that weekend, and Emily, who was a member of the junior high group, had looked forward to participating in it. Ann, a senior high member, not only attended but spoke. With Emily's permission, I left the hospital early Sunday morning to arrive in Staunton in time to attend worship and hear Ann's testimonial.

Ann has many gifts and talents. She's smart, confident, poised, and capable. She's also funny and seems to thrive on impromptu speaking. Spontaneous public speaking may well be her greatest strength. I know that she prepared at least some of her remarks for that Sunday morning, but her conclusion, which was about Emily's walk of faith, was spontaneous, eloquent, powerful, and deeply moving.

My spirit was stirred to its very core as Ann's words brought forth laughter and tears from the congregation. Emily would write in her diary that evening: "My mom said Ann was great. Everyone was crying by the end. They were crying about me. Oh well. I'll see ya tomorrow. So long. Bye Bye. Love, Emily Jones." How could I have two such remarkable children? To God be the glory. Amen.

Nearly seven years later, Ann would give another impromptu talk from the same pulpit, this one for Bubbles, who passed away on June 21, 2001. Originally, Bubbles's brother had agreed to say a few words about his oldest sister at her memorial service. However, just minutes before the service was to begin, he confessed that he simply could not go through with the task.

On the spot, Ann volunteered to speak in his place. With no more than ten or fifteen minutes to compose her thoughts, and without a single notecard, she walked to the pulpit and engaged every person present with her warm and loving memories of her Bubbles. Once again we laughed and cried as Ann spoke from the heart about this remarkable woman who, over the span of eighty-six years, touched many lives.

Years later, Ann would give yet another testimonial, this one before women present at her Wellspring Bible Study at West End Presbyterian Church in Richmond, Virginia. Ann spoke from her heart, sharing the story of her sister's journey through life to death. I have a CD copy of her message. Every word is spoken with deep love and respect for a sister whose life was far too short. I hope Ann will speak at my memorial service when the time comes. And I hope God grants me a little window to hear her when she does.

Chapter 9

I'm going to be in a magazine!
I'm very excited.

—Emily's diary,
July 8, 1994

In spite of the chemo, ulcers, and hospitalizations, the summer of 1994 was likely the best of Emily's life. Not only had she been featured on the Children's Miracle Network Telethon, she was psyched for her Make-A-Wish trip to the Walt Disney World Resort in August. She and her friends went to Staunton Braves baseball games at Moxie Stadium, located just two blocks from our house. They ate stadium hot dogs, drank sodas, and talked girl talk for hours on end. Her girlie group went shopping, to the movies, and swimming. Life felt normal, and it was sweet.

Emily was especially excited for Ann, who was joining other high school students and their chaperone for a week in France. Jerry and I were excited, too, but we definitely had a raised-eyebrow moment when, during a pretrip meeting, one of the girls from Ann's high school asked about the drinking age in France.

The group departed in late June, traveling by bus to the airport. My stomach churned as I watched Ann and the others drive away that day. Emily would write in her diary, "The whole day we were thinking of her because it was her first flight ever." Over the next eight days, I prayed many times for Ann's health and safety. After she got home, I knew my prayers had been answered as I listened to her tales of the French gentlemen who "insisted on buying our lunches" and her nonchaperoned, past-curfew jaunt to a Parisian nightclub with other high school travelers.

The day after Ann left for France, the rest of us traveled to UVA for the HEP's first quilt show. The Adolescent Quilting Project had been started in the early 1990s and quickly became very popular with both male and female teenage patients. Every quilt told a story or represented an important event in the life of its designer.

To me, Emily's fish quilt, with its bubbles and vibrant colors, spoke of her calm but free spirit. I don't think it had any sort of deep meaning. Perhaps it was a reminder of her own pet goldfish, which she'd won at her school's Halloween party when she was in second grade. Ann had won a fish, too, but the poor creature died the following day. Emily's fish, which she named Fish, adjusted to its new surroundings right away, swimming the limited perimeter of its glass house without any sign of illness or distress.

One summer day a year or two later, poor Fish jumped out of its bowl. I happened to be nearby and saw the suicidal leap into fresh air. I quickly grabbed Fish's slippery tail and dropped it, gulping air, back in the water. Thinking I'd have a little fun with Emily, who was outside when it happened, I told her that Fish had leaped out of the bowl and that I'd performed CPR to save its life. She believed me! "Emily," I laughed, "does Fish breathe air?"

She got her distinctive "Oh, Mom" look and went on her way. The next day, Fish's tail turned bright red where I had pinched it. Several days later, the red part fell off and I felt terrible. At least Fish didn't die. In fact, Fish outlived Emily by two years.

No sooner had Ann left for France than Emily busied herself getting ready for the Fourth of July celebration, which was a very big deal in Staunton. Staunton is the home of the much-loved country music group the Statler Brothers. Since 1970, they had graciously performed free concerts every July 4 as an incredible "give back" to their city. They put Staunton on the map. Actually, the concert was the culmination of Staunton's Happy Birthday Celebration, which lasted two days and included a vesper service, parade, and carnival.

By 1994, the event had grown unbelievably. That July, nearly 100,000 people packed Moxie Stadium to hear the quartet sing their greatest hits as well as gospel favorites. Because we lived less than two blocks away, we were expecting lots of family and friends to come for food, a clean restroom, and, most importantly, a place to park within easy walking distance of the stadium. Emily proudly wore blue-jean shorts and a new t-shirt with a logo celebrating twenty-five consecutive years of Statler Brothers concerts (1970–1994). Even if you weren't a country music fan, you couldn't live in Staunton and not feel pride in the Statlers.

Emily's 1994 decorations included a crisp American flag and red, white, and blue crepe paper streamers that were carefully wound on the front porch and fence. They were in place well before it was time to leave for the parade. In years past, she and Ann had set up lemonade stands on the front sidewalk in hopes of clearing a little pocket change to spend at the carnival, but with Ann away in France, Emily wasn't interested. She was expecting friends later in the day and wanted to spend as much time with them as possible. She didn't need money; Bubbles, PawPaw, and Jerry happily slipped her enough to pay for whatever she wanted.

By nine in the morning, we were ready to go to the parade. Once at the park, we found a great place in the shade for our folding chairs. Antique cars came first, followed by city officials and beauty queens on floats. Schools were not in session, so there were only a few marching bands. Of course, the main attraction was the float carrying the Statler Brothers.

After the parade ended, we returned home to make final preparations for the arrival of friends and family. First to arrive were

Jerry's parents, his sister and her husband (Carol and Sam), and Sam's son, Alan. Sam always brought firecrackers—not anything too dangerous, just the little things that smoke and crackle and unfurl like snakes in the grass. The kids loved them. And, of course, when it got dark, everyone waved sparklers.

Ravenous appetites were satisfied by early afternoon as we filled our plates with all manner of delicious picnic fare. Emily's friend Monika and her family had also arrived, and there was much chatter and fellowship on the back patio. The day was hot but gorgeous. Emily had baked and decorated an "Old Glory" cake, based on a picture she had seen in a magazine. She iced her yellow cake with white frosting, then used blueberries for stars and strawberries for stripes. It was delicious and earned her plenty of compliments. Best of all, she could have her cake and eat it, too.

By midafternoon, the side yard looked more like a parking lot than a play area. It was large enough to hold about twenty vehicles, but this year we squeezed in twenty-three. One year, we had complete strangers pull in along with invited guests. The driver explained that one of his passengers—maybe his mother or wife—had a heart condition and couldn't walk far. That man may or may not have been telling the truth; regardless, Jerry allowed him to leave his car. We'd heard that the previous owners actually let their children charge people to park cars in the yard. I guess it was a good way for them to earn a little spending money, but we couldn't bring ourselves to do it. Somehow it just didn't seem right to ask for money on a day when we were celebrating *free*dom.

Not everyone went to the park. Bubbles used a walker and lacked the physical stamina to walk any distance or manage herself in large crowds. She enjoyed playing hostess at home, especially when her brother and his family came, along with Louise, a good friend from church. They would sit in the cool shade of the porch and chat or simply watch as streams of people paraded down the front sidewalk on their way to the carnival or stadium. Announcements on the PA system at Moxie Stadium were easy to hear, so Bubbles and others could easily tell what was going on two blocks away. Country music bands played all afternoon, providing entertainment for all the stay-at-homes.

Those of us who braved the afternoon sun to walk to the park didn't stay long. Of course, Emily charmed PawPaw into going to the carnival. In all likelihood, he was the one most eager to go, as there was a lot of kid in him. I don't think Emily rode any rides, but I'm sure she got a funnel cake and played a game or two before coming home.

By dusk, eager fans were filling the tightly packed rows of folding chairs that covered the baseball diamond and surrounding area. Within a few minutes, the crowd started a low and excited rumble as the Statler Brothers' band began testing their sound equipment. Soon after, a sea of fans was hearing what they came for, and they went wild, clapping and cheering with every song.

Some years, summer storms interrupted the festivities. This summer's evening was just about as perfect as you can get in Virginia in July—hot but not oppressive, with plenty of lightning bugs seeming to dance to the beat of the music. Around ten o'clock, the Statlers sang their last encore and thanked everyone for coming. Fireworks started immediately. Mature trees in our neighborhood blocked much of the display, but we heard every crackle and pop.

By shortly after eleven, all of our guests had gone home. The streets were emptied of cars, and only isolated backyard firecrackers disturbed the quiet. Emily was exhausted but still feeling the natural high of a very fun day. After all, she had been able to eat, was surrounded by family and friends, went to the parade, made a couple of trips to the park, and lived every minute to the fullest. We could not have hoped for anything better. UVA Hospital was a million miles from our thinking.

When Jerry and I had moved to Alleghany Avenue in 1983, we'd had no idea that we would have such good neighbors or that the neighborhood itself would be full of little girls about the same age as our two. Bob and Margie Moore lived directly across the street. They didn't have children, unless you count their cat and dog as children (as they did).

Sydney was a wonderful border collie—smart, energetic, and friendly. Bob and Margie even had birthday parties for her, including one with a candy-stuffed parrot piñata held in our backyard! Bob and Margie not only had great pets, they were great conversationalists and even better cooks. Occasionally, on warm summer evenings, they would invite us to join them on their back patio for snacks and wine. Lazy evenings such as those were a great deal of fun.

The Thompsons lived next door to Bob and Margie. At that time, they had two little girls. Tara, the older, was a couple of years younger than Emily. Living next to the Thompsons were the Zimmermans, who had four daughters. Heidi, who was the youngest, was Ann's age. Over time, Ann, Heidi, Tara, and Emily formed a wonderful little friendship quartet. They spent many happy hours together during the Alleghany Years. Summertime found them in each other's homes almost daily and for sleepovers at night. They put on plays, ran lemonade stands, rode bicycles, and swam. Only rarely did we hear complaints of boredom.

Heidi even went on vacation with us. Both of my girls loved her dearly. She didn't mind sitting in the middle of the back seat and somehow kept everyone, including Jerry and me, happy on long road trips. One year, we were on our way to Chincoteague on Virginia's Eastern Shore when Heidi got chicken pox. Of course, we had to turn around and go home. Even at age thirty-six, Heidi still remembers the vacation that wasn't.

Heidi's family also took Ann with them to the beach several times. They always went to Duck, North Carolina. Mr. Z, as he was fondly called, was a great teaser. He still laughs about the time he scared Ann silly by telling her he'd seen a shark swimming nearby. She took refuge on a small sandbar, too terrified to leave its safety.

Several years before Emily became ill, Heidi went with us on a bus trip to the Macy's Thanksgiving Day Parade in New York City. We were on the bus all night, arriving in the predawn hours of Thanksgiving. The girls and I had managed to get a little sleep, but Jerry got none. Dawn found us exploring the chilly streets near our hotel while the sun inched slowly above the skyscrapers. Eventually we had breakfast, then staked out our spot to watch the parade.

Watching the Macy's Thanksgiving Day Parade on television is one thing, but seeing it live is an entirely different experience. The giant helium balloons are absolutely incredible in real life. Watching the volunteer crew maneuver the huge inflatables through the narrow, wind-tunnel streets provides plenty of thrills, and we quickly became part of unanimous cheers when a sudden wind gust would send a balloon careening against the side of a building as its handlers struggled to control the impact.

Boyz II Men were featured in "our" Macy's parade. I thought the girls might float off the planet when the group rode by, waving to a musical backdrop of one of their wildly famous songs. Jerry and I gave a big thumbs up to the Addams Family float. Waving to Lurch, Cousin It, Grandma, Wednesday, and Pugsley was a way cool experience.

Thursday night, our group had tickets for a Broadway production of *The Secret Garden*. Unfortunately, we were in the "cheap seat" section and saw mostly the tops of actors' heads. The music was fantastic, however.

We used Friday to explore as much of NYC as possible, starting with an organized tour that included a stop in Chinatown. It was here in one of the small shops that Emily purchased a parasol and a pair of pretty black shoes that had flowers embroidered on them. Both items are stored in a tub in the attic. One day, we'll give them to our older granddaughter, who is Emily's namesake.

The tour also included a visit to the public observation level (107th floor) of the World Trade Center South Tower. Poor Jerry couldn't look down to the streets far below us. Our formal tour ended with a walk in Central Park followed by a delicious meal at the famous Tavern on the Green.

After lunch, we returned to our hotel, then set out from there to roam the nearby streets. Emily insisted on stopping at nearly every vendor and even bought a ten-dollar Bettie Boop sweatshirt from one. I was sure it would disintegrate the first time it was washed, but instead it held up well through many washings.

What would a trip to New York be without a visit to FAO Schwartz? The girls had seen the movie *Big,* starring Tom Hanks, and knew well the scenes that took place in the famous toy store. The distance between our hotel and FAO Schwartz was too far to walk, so Jerry decided to hail a cab. I basically went into a panic when the cabbie said he could take no more than four people. My separation anxiety demanded that we ride together.

The poor driver must have realized my distress and said he would take us, provided one of the girls would "disappear" in the back seat. Emily was the smallest, so she was elected to stretch flat across our laps while Jerry rode in the front seat. Every few blocks, her head popped up only to have me push it back down. She was a good sport, and our driver didn't receive a ticket. Frankly, he deserved a medal for saving me from a panic meltdown. Visiting FAO Schwartz was worth the effort, too.

Friday night, we walked to Radio City Music Hall by way of Rockefeller Center. It seemed that street musicians were performing on every block. Their music was infectious and fun. While all of us enjoyed it, Emily absolutely absorbed it. One of Jerry's happiest memories is of her "dancing with joy" along the streets of New York.

Once at Radio City Music Hall, we had great seats for the Christmas Spectacular, which featured the famed Rockettes and concluded with a live nativity. Weary but determined to squeeze in every possible tourist opportunity, we joined our tour director for a late-evening visit to the Empire State Building. The trip required a subway ride, which was fun. Atop the Empire State Building, the November air was cold and crisp, but it was also clear, and our nighttime view of the NYC skyline was spectacular.

Saturday was a free day, and we used it to tour the Statue of Liberty. Rastafarians playing steel drums mesmerized us as we waited for a boat to transport us to the statue. For a claustrophobic person like me, climbing the Statue of Liberty was anything but exciting. There were two staircases—one ascending and one descending. With so many visitors, every step had a person on it such that the line moved in unison with *no way to turn around.*

There were little landings along the way, and, in case of emergency, a single-rider elevator occupied a center shaft. I could see daylight through cracks in Lady Liberty's dress, which made me question the statue's stability. I'm glad I climbed to the top and peered out of the windows beneath her crown, but I couldn't get back to the base soon enough.

Saturday afternoon, we visited the Lincoln Center Gift Shop. Emily purchased a lovely Christmas ornament featuring a scene from *The Nutcracker.* That night, we went with the full group for dinner at a popular Italian restaurant. Immediately afterward, we boarded our bus for the long drive home. That trip remains one of our all-time favorites.

Sleepovers were common events at our house. In the 1980s, very few families had VCRs, so Jerry would visit a local movie store, rent a machine, and select a kid flick for the girls to watch. Giggles and chatter could be heard late into the night. Those were fun, carefree times. In fact, my favorite picture of the four best friends was taken one summer day in our backyard.

Emily was five or six years old. The girls were sitting on our picnic table, their legs crossed in the same direction and their arms around one another. Everyone was smiling and content. Looking back many years later, we realize how blessed we had been to live in a neighborhood where lifelong friendships were forged. Truly, those were the best of times with the best of friends.

Before Emily got sick, Tara and her family moved to a new, larger house south of Staunton. While they didn't see as much of each other as they would have liked, the girls remained good friends. We were all delighted the Monday afternoon that Tara, her mom, two sisters, and new brother made a surprise hospital visit to Emily, who at that time was still recovering from her first two surgeries. The girls even appeared with Emily on the HEP's closed-circuit television show, *Confetti*.

Tara's mom, a Tupperware representative, brought Emily a special gift—an adorable, stuffed, soft and cuddly white seal with big black eyes. "Tuppie" became Emily's constant companion. They were separated only by death.

Eventually, our little circle of neighborhood friends went separate ways. The Thompsons moved out of state, the Zimmermans moved to another neighborhood, and the Moores moved to another town.

A friend loves at all times.

—Proverbs 17:17

Ann, Heidi, and Tara grew up and went to college. All three girls are now married and have beautiful children of their own. The remarkable thing is that after eighteen years, I remain in contact with these dear friends. And I know for sure that Emily is never far from their hearts.

School friends were also an important part of our girls' lives. Kadee Boone became one of Emily's best friends when they met in second grade. Randi, Kadee's mom, was a special education teacher in the same school where I taught and one of the funniest people I had ever met. She found humor in her students and in her teaching. Many an afternoon, I doubled over in laughter listening to Randi's summary of the day in her classroom. We were all devastated when Kadee's family moved to Georgia at the end of her fourth grade year. Emily and Kadee stayed in contact through letters, occasional phone calls, and summertime visits.

It was Emily's year to visit Kadee in 1994. We left Bubbles, Ann, Fish, and Emily's other pet, a solid-black dwarf rabbit named "Hook," at home and set off for Marietta on the morning of July 9. We could have made the trip in one day but decided to break it up into two, spending a night in Greenville, South Carolina. I remember watching the locally televised Miss South Carolina beauty pageant that night in the hotel room. Emily thought it was cool; Jerry thought it was boring.

Kadee is the second oldest of four sisters. Emily had always felt incredibly close to all of the Boones—and they to her. She used to tell Randi that she was going to move in with them when she finished college. Randi just laughed her southern laugh and said, "Well, honey, just come on." The funny thing is, I think Emily was absolutely serious. She had always felt as if she fit in the Boone family.

We arrived in Marietta in the sweltering heat of the following afternoon, and Emily immediately assumed her position as fifth daughter in this wonderful family. Undeterred by the heat, she joined in the family activities, going to a delightful performance of Korean music that night and staying up late to watch *Grumpy Old Men*. She went with Kadee to her babysitting job and for late afternoon swims.

One night they went to the movies to see *Forrest Gump*. Emily was deeply moved by this film. She would see it two more times during the summer and eventually purchased her own copy. It would play an important role on the last day she spent in our house.

The day before we were to leave, Jerry and I took Emily and Kadee to the Tennessee Aquarium in Chattanooga. Our tour started at the top of the building in an area that simulated the Tennessee River basin and included native freshwater fish and water fowl. From there we descended through a multitude of fish and turtle habitats, finally arriving at the sea, where freshwater meets saltwater. Our tour ended at a tank filled with huge sturgeons and other sea creatures. Because we were supposed to be in the deep ocean, the room was very dark and cold. The whole experience was mesmerizing. Emily rated the aquarium "cool," which was high praise, according to her adolescent vocabulary.

Our final outing was to Stone Mountain Park. Stone Mountain is just that—a huge quartz rock that stands more than sixteen hundred feet tall. On summer nights, it becomes the screen for an enormously popular laser show. Carloads of people toting lawn chairs, blankets, and coolers of food and drink unload shortly before dusk to await the event. It is truly spectacular, as laser horses, accompanied by loud music, gallop across the quartz surface. We certainly had never before seen anything like it. But what I remember far better than the laser show was the ride there from Marietta.

Just as we were leaving for Stone Mountain Park, a terrible storm erupted, with fierce lightning, window-rattling thunder, wind, and gray sheets of horizontal rain. All nine of us were packed into the big Boone van. Kadee's dad, Sandy, was driving. The interstate system around Atlanta boasts many lanes and very fast drivers. Cars whizzed past us, throwing water across the van and making it nearly impossible to see even with the wipers on high. I was scared, but I did my best not to show it. The crazy thing was, Sandy didn't seem at all nervous. His only concern was that the weather might make us late or would cancel the show altogether.

I failed to mention that the Boone family is incredibly musical. Their move to Staunton was so that Sandy could get his master's degree in "wind conducting" at nearby James Madison University.

At least three of the girls played instruments (Sandy always said Kadee was the best bassoonist in the state of Georgia) and they all sang. Randi's voice was performance quality.

So, on I-75 going who knows how fast in the middle of a severe thunderstorm, Sandy, Randi, Abby, Kadee, Jenny, and Nattie broke into song—something from *The Sound of Music*. The experience was simply heavenly. Absorbed in their spontaneous concert, I stopped worrying about my safety. The storm was history by the time we got to Stone Mountain, and the show went on as scheduled.

Emily sobbed when it came time for us to leave the next morning. Maybe she thought this was her last trip to Marietta and that she would never again be the fifth child in a family she loved so much. Perhaps she just missed her friend. She cried a long time that morning. Silent sobs filled my own heart.

The following Monday, Emily was back at the PCC to start her seventh round of chemo. Around the same time, an editor with a new magazine called *Girls' Life* had contacted the Hospital Education Program seeking a teenaged girl with cancer to write about her experiences. Marta approached Emily that afternoon and asked if she would like to write an article for publication. She accepted immediately. An interview with Kelly White, one of the magazine's editors, was scheduled for Wednesday.

That day came quickly. Emily went to the PCC for her chemo treatment as usual. She didn't feel great, but she never let on. She wore a blue dress with daisies on it. Visible above the neckline was the gauze pad that covered her port. She brought Cindy Wig and Pin Hat, as well as her favorite *Champion* baseball cap. By this time, Emily was completely at ease with being bald and wore Cindy only on special occasions. She most often wore the baseball cap, which was cooler and more comfortable.

Marta and Kelly arrived on schedule, and the three of them set off on a tour of the PCC and the seventh floor of University Hospital. This interview belonged to Emily. I knew she would have no problem talking about what it was like to live with cancer. Many pictures were taken that morning—some with Cindy and Pin Hat and some hairless with the *Champion* cap. Four appeared in the publication, and she looked radiant in all of them. Before Kelly left, she gave Emily a copy of volume 1, issue 1 of *Girls' Life* and told her that her article would appear in volume 1, issue 2. Emily could hardly wait to start writing. She would enter the world stage with this opportunity.

Within a few days, her article and a copy of her Valentine's poem were on their way to Kelly. Most of the article, which is reprinted on pages 243–45, was dedicated to explaining adenocarcinoma of the small bowel and its impact on her. Near the end, however, she made a point of saying that cancer wasn't an automatic death sentence. She also emphasized that she was a normal teenager who happened to have cancer. She concluded by thanking people for listening and reading her story. She invited readers to write to her. In anticipation that readers just might write, we got Emily her own post office box. That turned out to be a very wise decision.

Emily's Grandfather Jones (PawPaw) was much beloved in the family. He adored his granddaughters and was the consummate good sport with their antics. He turned sixty-eight that July. Because Emily's treatment schedule kept us fairly close to home, he and MeeMaw came to Staunton to celebrate the occasion with us. They arrived in the early afternoon and spent time laughing and talking.

Elmer loved to tell jokes, and he always had new ones to try on us. Emily, who loved pranks, saw his arrival as the perfect opportunity to administer the long-standing Jones tradition of buttering the birthday person's nose. She quietly approached him from the back and managed to smear a large dollop of butter on his proboscis, causing the room to erupt in laughter. Emily doubled over in laughter knowing she had pulled off the ultimate surprise. Elmer, who loved being the center of attention, beamed with delight.

A short while later, we went to dinner at a favorite restaurant. As she always did, Emily ordered liver and onions. A funny thing is that I craved liver and onions throughout my pregnancy with Emily and ate the grilled combination at least once or twice a month for nine months. Go figure.

The end of July saw us getting ready for our much-anticipated trip to the Walt Disney World Resort. Ann's sixteenth birthday would occur while we were in Florida. Unbeknown to her, David Motes, our good friend and trusted car salesman, had found a reliable used car, which we purchased as a birthday gift for her. The spunky Toyota Corolla was ready for pick up on July 29. Emily all but had "I've got a secret" written across her forehead. Knowing that she would not be able to hold it in until we returned from Orlando, we decided to celebrate Ann's birthday ahead of time.

After Ann had returned from France, she volunteered her time and talents to help with set design and construction for a local outdoor theater. She also assisted with props during performance week. Bob and Margie Moore produced the play and took Ann to the theater nightly. She usually got home late, which set the stage for Emily to pull off one of her best surprises.

Emily started working on the little blue car as soon as Jerry arrived home with it. By nightfall, it was decorated and awaiting Ann's return. Emily peered out the window overlooking the driveway as Ann whooped and laughed at the discovery of her own vehicle.

Emily, who loved surprises more than food, was beside herself with the success of this one. I know she could hardly wait to ride solo with her big sister. Ann christened her little car Periwinkle; she and her wheels rolled together until she was a junior in college.

We held Ann's birthday celebration on August 1, five days ahead of the official date. That night, all of us gathered around the dining room table for dinner. When everyone had finished, Emily went to the kitchen to put the final touches on the birthday cake, which she then carried into the dining room, ablaze with sixteen candles. Emily's own birthday cake would never hold more than fourteen candles.

Also there that evening was Emily's friend Katie Propst, who had come to spend the night. They had been best friends since elementary school. Katie visited Emily many times during her hospitalizations, sometimes even staying the night. They would lie side-by-side in the hospital bed, watching television, eating, and talking teen talk. They went for walks around the seventh floor and built a strong, very special relationship.

Katie understood Emily as well as anyone. Sometimes I think they passed thoughts between them by osmosis. They were just that close. As heart-wrenching as it was for sweet Katie to watch cancer consume her dear friend, she remained by Emily's side until the end. Today she is an elegant, eloquent, poised woman completing her residency in ob/gyn at a Philadelphia-area hospital. Shortly after Emily passed away she wrote:

> Emily changed my life. She had been my best friend since third grade. And suddenly, just like that, she was gone. . . . All throughout her illness she always had great determination that she would be healed and an extraordinary belief in God. Emily often told me and many others that she knew she was healed. Emily made me greatly value my life and others around me. I am now very grateful to her for teaching me that very valuable lesson for life. I think about Emily *every* day, and I still miss her

terribly. It [her death] was the hardest thing that I have ever had to deal with in my life. But I can still say that I was extremely happy to be a part of such a wonderful experience, but even happier to have known someone full of such love, determination, wisdom, and kindness.

Emily's Make-A-Wish trip began on August 5 with a flight she, Jerry, Ann, and I took from Roanoke, Virginia, to Orlando, Florida. She was between treatments and free of mouth ulcers. Quite literally, she was set to have the time of her life. The drive to Roanoke is a blur, and I only vaguely remember the flight from there to Charlotte, where we changed planes.

The flight from Charlotte to Orlando International Airport was more memorable, as we encountered turbulence near the end. Sitting in the tail section, we bounced like ping-pong balls. I distinctly remember looking out the window at huge, white thunderheads towering all around us. We circled around and through them until we were cleared to land. I was tremendously relieved to plant my feet on *terra firma* that afternoon.

The entire Disney trip, including car rental and spending money, was paid for by Make-A-Wish. As promised, we were met by volunteers—a husband and wife team—as we exited the Orlando Airport gate. They had a pair of Make-A-Wish sunglasses and a Mickey Mouse stuffed toy for Emily. They accompanied us to luggage pick-up, then to the car rental office, all the while sharing tips for making our week as magical as possible.

Soon we had keys to a roomy Ford Taurus station wagon and were on our way to Give Kids The World Village (GKTW), a resort-like place in Kissimmee created to bring joy, happiness, and magic to children with life-threatening illnesses and their families.

At the guest relations building, which today is known as the House of Hearts, we learned that they were filled to capacity, and we would be housed at Holiday Inn East, also in Kissimmee. We were invited to participate in all activities and meals at the Village, however.

Before heading to the hotel, we were given a packet containing our tickets to the Walt Disney World Resort and other area attractions, parking passes, etc. We were also loaned a video camera, then received a copy of our videotape on the last day of our vacation.

An impressive list of activities had been planned for Emily. Of course, three days at Walt Disney World Resort theme parks would be the highlight, but also included were tickets to Universal Studios, King Henry's Feast (a medieval dinner theater), and lunch at Hard Rock Cafe-Orlando. We would maintain a dizzying pace all week.

After settling in at our hotel, we returned for dinner at the Gingerbread House Restaurant, a cafeteria-style eatery with child-sized and adult tables, the tops of which were covered with mints—27,000 of them, in fact. A shelf lined the ceiling perimeter of the dining rooms and was filled with hundreds of dolls from all around the world. Volunteers served up trays with plenty of delicious food.

After dinner, we went to the ice cream caboose, a real train caboose painted bright red that was open at every mealtime—even breakfast—for anyone wanting a frozen sweet treat. Smiling volunteers dipped up *whatever* was ordered. Emily always got big scoops of vanilla in a cup. She then went to the topping station, where she piled on M&Ms, colored sprinkles, *lots* of cherries, and as much whipped cream as she could squeeze in the cup. She never finished eating one of her dessert masterpieces. In fact, with eyes bigger than stomachs, very few people did—and no one cared. The red caboose was about memory-making. It did its job well.

The Castle of Miracles was another really cool building at GKTW Village. Inside, it indeed looked like a castle, with painted stone walls and mysterious rooms. One room contained a grandfather clock called Father Time. Mostly, Father Time slept; his eyes were closed, and he whistled gently when he exhaled. He also had a long white beard. We saw Father Time with his eyes open only once—on the Mickey and Minnie "meet and greet" day.

Ann and Emily especially liked the castle room that was filled with drawers and doors that, when opened, made all sorts of sounds or played songs. One door sounded like a cricket chirping followed by a squeaky hinge followed by the *Hallelujah Chorus*. A wishing well was located in the same room. Drop in a coin and wait for a response. Emily and Ann liked it best when the well burped back at them.

Happy Harbor Fishing Pond was a fisherman's (or a would-be fisherman's) delight, as it was well stocked. Guests needed only to ask for a pole and some bait and head to the fishing area. Jerry, who is not an outdoorsman, cringed when Emily begged to go fishing. His best attempts to dissuade her failed and off we went to the pond, pole and supply of bread in hand. At least he didn't have to bait the hook with a worm. He confessed later that he'd prayed hard the fish weren't biting at that moment of the day. Jerry's prayers were answered; poor Emily never had so much as a nibble on her line.

Magic Kingdom was the first theme park we visited at the Walt Disney World Resort. We parked in the biggest lot I'd ever seen and headed for the ferry that would deliver us to the entrance. It was hot, but the boat ride across the lagoon was pleasantly cool and refreshing. We passed through the turnstile and made our way up Main Street, USA. Children laughed and tugged at their parents to walk faster. A beautiful but sweaty horse pulled a trolley packed with people, its bell clanging to clear the track ahead of it.

Before leaving our hotel that morning, Emily had pinned a big button with her name and "Give Kids The World" on her sleeveless blouse. "Cast members" in all three theme parks recognized it and either bumped Emily and Ann to the front of the line or sent them through the wheelchair entrance to avoid long lines. That was a really nice perk—sort of an early "fast track" system reserved for very special park visitors.

The magic of the Magic Kingdom enveloped us completely. We did as much as possible until the heat drove us back to our hotel for a rest, followed by dinner at GKTW. We were back on the Magic Kingdom ferry by sunset. While riding across the lagoon at dusk, we were treated to a magnificent Florida sunset. The sky was a deep orange-pink with huge clouds climbing like castle towers into the infinite sky. Main Street, USA was bright and alive. Cinderella Castle glimmered in the background, its high walls flooded in bright colors, while music poured from trees filled with twinkling lights.

Ten o'clock may well be the most magical hour during a summer night at the Magic Kingdom. Park lights dim and, just as the music peaks, Tinker Bell emerges from Cinderella Castle high above the crowd, which erupts in a thunderous cheer at her appearance. She floats above the crowd as thousands of cameras record every wave of her wand and children envision fairy dust sprinkling like glitter to the ground.

Since that night, Jerry and I have seen Tinker Bell exit the castle more than twenty times, and her magic is still the same. Perhaps it's because we hold dear the memory of that first night when we were a family of four who, if for only a short time, could put behind us the reality that at some point we would be a family of three.

Fireworks began almost immediately after Tinker Bell's flight. There are fireworks and there are *fireworks*. Until this night, the biggest display we had ever seen was in Bethlehem, Pennsylvania, in celebration of money raised by their school children to help restore the Statue of Liberty (Bethlehem children raised more money than any other children in the United States). Magic Kingdom fireworks are brilliantly synchronized, breathtaking, loud, and totally awesome—a pyrotechnic masterpiece. Today the Magic Kingdom fireworks pyrotechnic masterpiece is called "Wishes." It is even more brilliant, beautiful, and awesome. To this day, Jerry weeps every time he experiences it.

As the eleven o'clock hour approached, we left Cinderella Castle in search of curb seating to watch the SpectroMagic parade. Because of the late hour, many families had already left the park, so finding seating was easy. Jerry purchased battery-operated light-up roses for each of the girls, then he and the girls sat down to wait for the parade. I found a bench behind them and filmed all I could in the diminished light. The parade was absolutely awesome. Hundreds of thousands of lights covered every float. Even the characters' clothes were covered in dazzling lights.

Of course, Disney characters were the stars of the parade—Mickey, Minnie, Goofy, Cinderella, her prince, Alice in Wonderland, Chip and Dale, and many others. The highlight for Jerry was the appearance of Snow White and the Seven Dwarfs. I was filming and happened to catch one of the Dwarfs shaking Jerry's hand as he walked past. Seconds later, "Bashful" scooted by Emily, looked right at her, and gave her a sweet little wave. The moment was endearing. Jerry still talks about his handshake from a dwarf. Jiminy Cricket was the last character in the parade. He sat on a little stool saying, "So long. See you later."

The Magic Kingdom town clock was ready to strike midnight by the time we and several thousand additional exhausted souls left the park, having spent a nearly perfect day in a nearly perfect place. During the next two days, we park-hopped between Disney-MGM Studios, Epcot, and the Magic Kingdom. It was sunny, hot, and humid. Occasional storms would roll through, cool things off briefly, then it would heat back up.

Ann and Emily rode nearly every ride, sometimes multiple times. Star Tours in Disney-MGM Studios was one of Emily's favorites. She loved the way the "stars flew past you and made you think you were pushed back against the seat." The Tower of Terror was on their "must ride" list, but it moved to the "never again" side after just one terrorizing ride.

Jerry and I are not thrill seekers, but the Walt Disney World Resort has plenty of rides for people like us. As a family, we rode the Great Movie Ride, saw the Beauty and the Beast musical, and delighted in MuppetVision 3D, to name a few. By late afternoon, we were ready for rest and dinner at GKTW.

The second night, we went to Epcot (Experimental Prototype Community of Tomorrow). We were mostly interested in seeing IllumiNations, its spectacular fireworks and laser show. We were not disappointed. In fact, we enjoyed it so much that we returned late the next afternoon to do it all over again. Emily was completely mesmerized by Epcot's famous geodesic dome. I liked the dancing water. All of us enjoyed the performers at the various country pavilions around World Showcase lagoon, especially the Japanese drummers and Chinese acrobats.

That night, Epcot was open until one o'clock. Only we diehards were left at that hour. We had walked and walked and were near total exhaustion when Emily lobbied to visit one last gift shop. She was the sick one, but the rest of us ended up begging her to let us return to the hotel. We got there around two o'clock.

Fortunately, Emily could sleep in the next morning, since we had our meet-and-greet session with Mickey and Minnie at GKTW's Castle. I treasure the video taken that morning of Ann helping Emily put on her makeup. Sibling pettiness no longer existed between them; they simply enjoyed one another's company, and it was so sweet.

Jerry used to say that Ann picked and Emily whined. One Christmas when Ann was around twelve and Emily nine, they got into a nasty verbal spat. Jerry had had enough and said that, if he had only had the money, he would send them away to "Christmas camp." I recall vividly that Ann was standing beside me at the kitchen sink drying dishes. Without thinking, I looked at her and said, "You should have been an only child." Proverbs 18:21 (New Living Translation) says: "The tongue can bring death or life; those who love to talk will reap the consequences."

The words that slipped from my tongue that day have haunted me countless times over the ensuing years. I have peace that my words did not cause Emily's illness. They were spoken out of frustration. Yet, once spoken, they could never be retracted—only forgiven. I have asked for and received forgiveness for those words. I have forgiven myself, as well. On this day in a hotel room in Kissimmee, Florida, I was grateful beyond measure for the love that Ann and Emily shared and for their enjoyment in being together. Quite honestly, I cannot remember a single cross word between the two of them during the entire two years that Emily was ill.

After our Mickey and Minnie meet-and-greet session, we headed for Universal Studios. We took a neat tour of Nickelodeon Studios that included a live interactive show during which someone got slimed. We also took the Boneyard Tour, a tame ride through back lots containing props from previously released Universal films such as *Flight of the Navigator*. We rode Earthquake: The Big One, a ride on a NYC subway train that just happens to be underground when an 8.3 earthquake hits.

The biggest thrill was the special-effects water ride featuring the terrifying shark from *Jaws*. Our boat captain took us through several *Jaws* sets, then into a simulated harbor where the famed *Jaws* music started to play. A steamy mist suddenly covered the water and we knew that "it" was about to happen. Just as the music peaked, a huge shark lunged out of the water directly at us. Jerry screamed and I loved it! Actually, all of us screamed, got drenched, and laughed like crazy. It was so much fun.

Lunch that day was at the famed Hard Rock Cafe-Orlando, located at Universal Studios. The place was enormous, and its walls were covered with rock-and-roll memorabilia. The music was loud, but it was supposed to be. We each had huge lunches and dessert. Emily came away with a few new souvenirs and a very full tummy!

That night we had tickets for dinner at King Henry's Feast—a dinner theater of sorts where we had to bang our silverware on the table and sing "Bring on the next remove" to get the various courses. The entertainment was lively and fun and full of leaping ladies and medieval fare. Once again, we ate and ate, including more dessert. There were no trips to the red caboose that evening! Our dream week in Florida was almost over.

Early the next morning, we packed for our return home. We stopped at GKTW to pick up our video, eat breakfast, and take a last look around. Leaving that incredible resort was hard on many levels. Hardest was having to face the reality that Emily had a terminal illness. She would not again return to GKTW Village, but she did leave behind a little piece of herself.

Earlier in the week, she had been invited to write her name on a small mirror in the shape of a star. Her star was placed on a ceiling in the Castle beside hundreds of others bearing the names of Wish children who had visited the Village. Twinkling little stars in heaven—what a wonderful way to honor children with life-threatening diseases. Emily has a real star; it came to me some years after she passed away. It's the last star in the handle of the Big Dipper. Think of her the next time you see it, and she'll twinkle a wink back at you.

Chapter 10

I'm famous. Kind a cool. Don't you think?

—Emily's journal,
October 5, 1994

We flew home on Wednesday, August 10. Four days later, we were off to the Jones/Hutchison reunion. This family gathering, which had happened every second Sunday of August for more than sixty years, was a wonderful time of fellowship, delicious food, and remembrances.

Jerry, who has researched his family tree since he was in middle school, always took along his genealogical notebooks so that he could answer questions and update information on the spot. Now he does everything on a computer. Back then, everything was written by hand. Emily shared Jerry's fondness for genealogy. It is likely that she would have become the next "keeper of the keys."

Following lunch, much of the family reconvened at Jerry's grandfather's farm. Ann and Emily loved this part of the day the most, a feeling I shared. Cousins would play their guitars and sing, while others danced. Like a lot of country folks, they all knew how to flatfoot. Sometime during the afternoon, Jerry and I nearly always took a break to hike into the corn field to hunt for arrowheads. August wasn't the best time to go looking, since the corn was high and scratchy, but we tried anyway. Sometimes we got lucky and would find a flint point sticking up through the dirt and weeds.

Over the years, Jerry's arrowhead collection had grown to an impressive six hundred specimens, from tomahawks and scraping tools to many styles of flint points. According to a friend and authority on Native American artifacts, some of the arrowheads are up to twelve thousand years old, while others are relatively new. They were left behind by Native Americans who migrated through the high valley until they permanently left the area after the French and Indian War.

All afternoon, music and laughter could be heard coming from the farm on Sinking Creek. The children, including Ann and Emily, played in the creek and hunted crayfish under rocks. Around dusk, another huge spread of country food appeared on long tables in the side yard, including steaming, fresh-from-the-garden corn on the cob. Most people stayed to talk for a while after dinner, but once the evening air started to turn cool—and it nearly always did—family and friends shook hands or hugged and said they'd be back again next year. We returned home with full stomachs and memories to last a lifetime.

The day after the reunion, Emily started her final round of chemo. We drove to the PCC as usual, and her port was accessed. She chattered nonstop to every doctor and nurse who came into her clinic room about her Most Fabulous Ever Wish Trip. The following Friday, she finished her eighth round of 5-FU. It was over. Exploratory surgery to determine the status of her cancer would be scheduled for mid-October. Except for several outpatient medical tests, Emily would enjoy a nearly three-month reprieve from the hospital admissions and clinic appointments that had dictated how we'd lived our lives since the beginning of 1994.

Also during August, my prayer warrior friend, Karen, contacted me about an evangelist who was to be a speaker at a Christian women's group that she attended. She invited me to go with her but also said that the speaker and his wife would be happy to come to our house after the meeting to talk and pray with us privately. I asked Emily, who was comfortable with the latter plan.

The morning our visitors were to arrive dawned hot and sunny. When the doorbell rang, I was surprised to see not only Karen and the couple but three others standing on our porch. Emily took one look and dashed to the back of the house. Receiving prayers from strangers was not especially easy for Emily, and I understood why she fled. Yet they had come for a specific purpose, and I hoped that Emily might come forward with some coaxing. She did, and she listened as one of the group witnessed to us about having been healed of cancer some years earlier.

Then the evangelist asked if he could pray for Emily. She reluctantly agreed. He placed his right hand on her shoulder and began to recite a prayer from deep inside his soul. Over and over again he repeated, "The virtue of Jesus is passing into you." As I stood beside Emily, I became fully aware of the presence of the Holy Spirit in our living room. The feeling was tangible—real—and I was utterly convinced that Emily had been healed. I even expected the scars from her surgeries to be gone.

The evangelical entourage left shortly after. I asked Emily if I could peek at her belly. Nothing was different. I was mystified. To

> Is anyone among you sick?
>
> He should call the elders of the church to pray over him
>
> and anoint him with oil in the name of the Lord.
>
> And the prayer offered in faith will make the sick person well;
>
> the Lord will raise them up.
>
> *—James 5:14–15*

this day, I don't know what happened that hot August morning. What does it mean for the "virtue of Jesus" to pass into you? I am satisfied that whatever happened was spiritual and unseen by human eyes. I know that I stood in the presence of the Holy Spirit.

෴

Emily started eighth grade soon after Labor Day. Her classes included language arts, civics, Latin I, algebra, science, physical education, and chorus. After a few days, she noted in her diary, "I am starting to get the hang of going to classes again." In fact, she had missed more than sixty days of the second half of seventh grade. No wonder she was a little nervous about her new school year. She really liked her teachers and didn't mind that she had homework right out of the starting gate.

Emily and Katie also signed up for cheerleading for Buffalo Gap Little League. By the time school started, they had already been practicing for several weeks. Their first football game was on September 10. Gap beat the opposing team 38–0. Emily was so excited, and I was thrilled to see her having a good time. She wore her *Champion* hat and black and gold cheerleading outfit. Her hair was growing ("from fuzzy to spike," according to Jerry), and she felt good. Life seemed deliciously normal.

Emily also returned to some of her favorite church activities. She loved helping with "children and worship," a Bible-study program held during the worship hour. She truly enjoyed being around children and was good at child management. She was active in United Methodist Youth Fellowship and would be elected president of the junior high group later in the month.

During September, Emily continued cheerleading practice, school, homework, and sleepovers with girlfriends. On September 16, she went to a welcome-back dance at her middle school. Two weeks later, she went to another dance. Of course, I heard none of the details. When she arrived home, Jerry was sitting in the recliner at the back door waiting for her and asked if she'd had a good time. Emily burst into tears. She told him that no boy would dance with her because she was going to die. Emily left and went upstairs to her room. Jerry was so terribly upset that he got in the car and drove around for many hours.

Years later, I found an entry in her diary about the dance. She wrote not one word about her own heartbreak, just that she hadn't danced with anyone but had gotten up her nerve to ask "Chris" to dance with Monika.

On October 3, a big envelope arrived in the mail. The return address said it was from the editor of *Girls' Life*. Even though it was addressed to Emily, I could not stand the suspense and opened it. Inside was a copy of volume 1, issue 2 of the magazine, along with a letter from Kelly White, who apologized that it had taken a little longer than expected to send Emily's copy. She went on to say:

> Look at the pretty faces on Page 20! I'm so sorry about the typo (first column, second to the last paragraph). It's all my fault! I was proofing at 4 a.m. and totally blew it! Hope we're still friends.☺ Please, feel free to tell everyone it was *my* mistake (and you have this letter to prove it). I hope you are happy and feeling well.
>
> Take care, sweetie

I simply could not wait for Emily to get home from school that afternoon. I grabbed the envelope and drove to the middle school, stopping by the post office on the way. Much to my surprise, there was a letter in her box. I opened the box and took it out. I felt giddy with excitement. Once at her school, I asked the secretary to call her out of class. When Emily came into the office, I held up her magazine and fan letter without uttering a sound or cracking a smile. Words can't describe the look on her face. It was so, so wonderful.

Fan letters started to arrive daily in Emily's box. She could hardly wait to go to the post office each afternoon. Over the next six months, she received hundreds of letters from girls around the world. Some wrote multiple times. Emily took it all in stride. In the beginning, she tried to write individual responses, but she was soon too overwhelmed to keep up with the volume of letters, so resorted to a form letter. Virtually every letter she received expressed concern for her health and made a statement about her bravery, making clear to us that Emily had stepped into the lives and hearts of teens around the globe.

One letter in particular sticks with me. It was written by a young lady who lived in Canada. She happened to come across a copy of *Girls' Life* in her school library, read Emily's article, and decided to write. Her name was Emily; her brother's name was Isaac. Emily and Isaac—I could not get over the coincidence. I still think about them from time to time and wonder what the adult Emily and Isaac from Canada are like.

Emily even received fan mail from UVA folks. The Benjamin Armistead Shepherd Professor and Chair at UVA Children's Medical Center wrote, "I had an opportunity to read your article in *Girls' Life* magazine. It is a wonderful message and you should be very proud of this accomplishment. We are delighted that you are part of the CMC family." Jerry and I were touched by this letter.

Emily also got a lovely letter from Ann Hamilton, whose mother, Mary, lived across the street from us. Ann is an accomplished television producer and writer who, in 1991, was nominated for two Emmy Awards for her work on *thirtysomething*. We were unaware that Mary had sent Emily's article to her daughter until Emily received Ann's letter. Ann wrote:

I thought your story was very moving, you sound very courageous for a 13-year-old. I liked the poem, too. Are you keeping a diary? Do you want to be a writer one day? I'm a writer and sometimes it's really rewarding. . . . I wrote a "thirtysomething" episode about miscarriage and we got a lot of mail saying "Thanks for understanding." Your article does the same thing, it helps explain something a lot of people don't understand.

Emily was required to keep a journal for her eighth-grade language arts class. In it, she wrote candidly about her approaching exploratory surgery: "I am getting anxious because the hospital is going to call. They are going to tell me when I get a CT scan and will have surgery. I will miss some school but it is worth it. I will be unable to do things I enjoy. I won't do ballet, cheerleading, and play sports. I will be very sad but my friends will cheer me up. In the end it will be worth it."

Once she learned the dates of her tests, she rationalized their impact on her life: "I would really just like to get the tests over. I won't be able to eat for a while till the tests are over. Oh well I need to get used to it. I will have tests the rest of my life."

Her entry at the end of September clearly described how much she disliked drinking the "chalky milkshake" and "fizzy stuff" but again rationalized their importance: "I guess it's worth knowing they can see inside of me instead of having to live not knowing if I am cured or not. So in the end it's all worth it." She wrote at the end of the same entry: "My tests were good. So all is well."

Emily was admitted to the hospital for exploratory surgery on October 13. She had a CT scan, requiring her to drink the yucky liquid, and, on top of that, a nasal tube was inserted. She went into surgery early the next morning and was in recovery by early afternoon. Jerry and I waited nervously for Dr. McGahren to give us a report on her cancer. He met us with good and bad news:

The cancer had not spread, but there were still hundreds of small tumors; the two that he biopsied were both "live" cancers.

Dr. Dunsmore spoke with us as well. She presented us—including Emily—with five options: go to St. Jude's to enter their trials, stay at UVA and try a new drug, continue more rounds of 5-FU, go to Johns Hopkins for their new study, or do nothing. Johns Hopkins was eliminated immediately because Emily was too young to participate. Additionally, Johns Hopkins would not allow participation if there was progression of disease. I suppose live cancer cells constituted progression of disease.

We were prepared to do any of the options, but we left the decision up to Emily. She wrote in her school journal: "Well I made my choice after a while of thinking. I decided to continue with the same chemo I had been taking. I think I made a very good decision. The doctor said any decision is a good decision. I think I made the best one I could of." She opted to repeat her 5-FU therapy. At least she knew what the side effects would be.

Not long after Emily's surgery and the confirmation that cancer was still present, I received another letter from Karen Hays, my steadfast prayer warrior. She wrote:

> I know it was a great disappointment and set back to find those nodules still present. However, my spirit still has great peace about Emily's healing. The faithfulness of God is ever present. . . . The Lord has not encouraged you to this point to bring it to a close—NO—There is much left to be done and it will be done in HIS timing. . . . You know not how many lives you have touched or will be touched. The Lord is using your faithfulness and witness to bear witness of Himself. So when we ask Why? . . . remember there is a bigger picture and you know not who else you are to touch. . . . Although your spirit may be heavy now, there will come a time of praise and rejoicing if we don't grow weary in well doing. . . . He will honor your faithfulness and your witness for Him. . . . You know I pray for all of you without ceasing.

Emily was admitted to the hospital for her first dose of 5-FU on October 31—just in time to attend the HEP's annual Halloween party. Auntie Ann, who was visiting from Pennsylvania, accompanied me to the party. Katie, who was looking forward to the party almost as much as Emily, was there, too. In fact, she and Emily had planned their costumes well in advance—each decorated a cardboard box to look like a die, and together they were a pair of dice ("paradise").

Auntie Ann, Katie, and Emily laughed and talked and participated in Halloween activities. All of us had a terrific time. I have said many times since Emily was sick that, if she had to be sick, I am grateful that she was sick during the HEP's pinnacle years of normalizing hospitalizations for patients. These activities were indeed fun, but, more importantly, they were memory makers. It is quite probable that some of the children at that party did not live to enjoy another Halloween.

In no time, Emily's mouth was ravaged by ulcers. I took her to the clinic at the PCC three days after she finished her first round of chemo, but she resisted admission and was sent home with pain medication. The next day, I took her to the seventh floor to participate in a live interview for FX, a New York–based television station. She was in considerable discomfort and asked to see a doctor when the television segment was completed. She was admitted right away.

Pumped full of morphine, Emily was groggy and didn't remember much of the next several days. In fact, continuing admissions had begun to take a toll on her. Later, she referenced this admission in her school journal, saying that she was tiring of being in the hospital. "I was getting depressed."

As it happened, Jerry arrived for a visit and was able to cheer her up. She lobbied her doctors until they allowed her to go home. She stayed home the next day but was in school the day after and was so happy to be among her friends once again.

The immune-boosting injections were to continue as part of Emily's second course of 5-FU treatment. Initially, she was told that she needed to learn to do self-injections. She tried but was never able to plunge the needle into her own thigh (she wrote repeatedly in her diary about the level of pain caused by these shots). We had a nurse from Home I.V. Care, Susan Shipp (whose own two sons were Emily's classmates), and it was arranged for her to do them.

Emily missed many days of school during November. I got her assignments, and she kept up as she was able, whether in the hospital or at home. She started a second round of 5-FU on November 28, finishing it on December 2.

Amazingly, Emily managed to help with Staunton Academy of Ballet's 1994 production of *The Nutcracker*. She was assigned "child management," which meant she helped the youngest children stay in one place between scenes, as well as get on stage at the appropriate time. It was simple work, but she loved it. I don't remember Emily expressing any self-pity over not being on stage herself. She was completely content behind the scenes.

Thank goodness Emily's mouth ulcers were gone by Christmas. Jerry and I had planned a return trip to the Walt Disney World Resort for Emily, her friend Kadee Boone, and Bubbles. Arrangements with Kadee's parents were made well in advance, and four-day park-hopper tickets were delivered to our house, ready for opening on Christmas Eve. Ann, who was a member of her high school volleyball team, opted out of this trip so that she could play in several holiday tournaments. She made arrangements to stay with friends while we were gone. She was also dating a classmate named Andy, who was a definite draw on her time.

After attending Christmas Eve services, we came home for a little party with our neighbors Bob and Margie Moore. It was nice having them celebrate with us, especially when Emily discovered the Walt Disney World Resort tickets. They weren't a complete surprise, but she didn't know many specific details of the trip. She sat on the living room couch wearing her church clothes and her black velvet hat (she was losing her hair once again). She looked adorable. Once she saw the tickets, she fanned them out in her hand with a look so expressive and excited that it sticks with me to this day.

Christmas morning, we packed the van and left for Georgia. Bubbles, who had always said she had no interest in going to Walt Disney World Resort, was as excited as Emily. She enjoyed staying in the Boones' lovely home and seeing Emily interact with their family. Although we were on the road again early the next morning, it still took a long time to get to Orlando due to major traffic snarls along the way, and it was well after dark when we checked into our rented condo.

The next morning, at Bubbles's request, we visited Cypress Gardens. My sister and I were in our teens when we had first gone there, so this trip was purely nostalgic. We watched the famed water skiers and strolled through the gardens, still lush in late December. We discovered a huge, magnificent display of poinsettias stacked to look like a giant red Christmas tree. Even Kadee and Emily were impressed. By early afternoon, we were back at the condo with plans to go to Magic Kingdom that evening. Beware the best-laid plans of mice and men.

Deciding we were low on towels, Jerry and I headed for the pool area where extras were available. I was wearing a long skirt and at the same time had new bifocals. Walking along, I failed to see a small rise in the stone sidewalk and, in an instant, fell face first onto the pebbled surface. I was a bloodied mess when I sat up, and I could feel my upper lip swelling rapidly. Jerry offered to take me to the ER, but I didn't think that was necessary.

Upon entering the condo, I went to the kitchen sink and splashed cold water on my very fat lip. Emily came running up to me and put her arm around me, "Go ahead and cry, Momma. It's okay.

You'll feel better if you cry." Those words came from the same person who would make me leave the room if I shed tears for her.

In 1994, the Walt Disney World Resort required a picture ID on tickets ordered through outside agencies such as AAA. We were in this category and, before we could enter the Magic Kingdom, we waited for the college-age attendant to ask us to "stand on the spot and smile." When my turn came, she got a rather surprised look on her face and asked what had happened to me. Jerry never missed a beat. With a totally straight face, he replied with amazing conviction, "I hit her."

I thought the poor girl would call the police on the spot. Jerry immediately said he was joking, and I backed him up. I can laugh at the picture now. Between my fat lip and big glasses, I look like a bug from outer space. All I needed were antennae.

For the next three days, we lived it up at the Walt Disney World Resort, hopping between the Magic Kingdom, Disney-MGM Studios, and Epcot. Bubbles used her wheelchair the whole time, which meant she went everywhere we did. There was more thrill seeker in my mom than I'd imagined. She avoided fast rides or those with sharp twists and turns but loved the tame ones and the wonderful shows, especially at Epcot. Most of all, she delighted in being with Emily and Kadee, absorbing their energy, joy, and excitement.

Emily and Kadee loved being together. They rode rides until we had to make them leave. It was a terrific holiday for all of us. In hindsight, did Emily know she would never return? Did she savor every second as a treasure that only she could store up?

We left Orlando on New Year's Eve, arriving in Marietta in plenty of time to bring in the New Year with the Boones. We lit sparklers and celebrated in grand style. Emily got to be the fifth Boone daughter one last time. On New Year's Day, we drove home. Emily was content, feeling good, and ready to start the second semester of eighth grade.

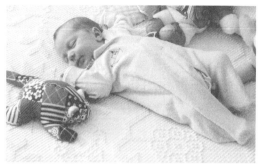

Emily Caroline Jones
at two months of age

Cabbage Patch buddies Heidi Zimmerman,
Shannon Mowry, Ann Jones, and Emily Jones

Neighborhood best friends Ann Jones, Emily Jones,
Tara Thompson, and Heidi Zimmerman

Emily stands beside
a small nativity set
that she arranged.

Emily's surprise
nativity made using
her favorite dolls

Emily and good friend
Monika Huffer

Emily blows out the candles
on her thirteenth-birthday cake.

Emily, Auntie Ann, and Ann stand in our side yard (May 1994). Emily's hair was noticeably thinning.

Robert Van Winkle interviews Emily at the Children's Miracle Network Telethon (June 1994).

Emily proudly displays her flag cake (July 4, 1994).

Emily butters PawPaw Elmer's nose on his sixty-eighth birthday.

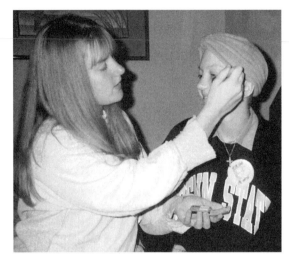

Ann applies Emily's makeup while on our Make-A-Wish trip.

Emily cheers for the Buffalo Gap Little League football team (fall 1994).

Ann, Jerry, and Emily help celebrate Bubbles's eightieth birthday.

Katie Propst and Emily pose as a pair of dice at the hospital Halloween party (October 31, 1994).

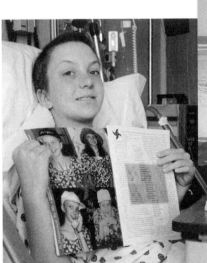

Lynn Woodson chats with Emily at the hospital Halloween party.

Emily and Ann prepare to ride their bicycles on Kiawah Island beach (March 1995).

Emily shows off her copy of *Girls' Life* from her hospital bed (fall 1994).

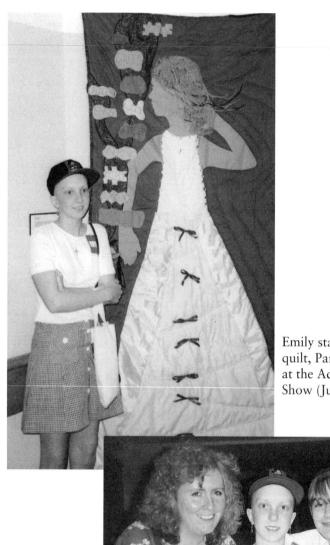

Emily stands beside her quilt, Pandora's Box, at the Adolescent Quilt Show (June 1995).

Nurse clinician Janet Stewart, Emily, and Katie Propst (June 1995)

Kadee Boone and Emily (July 1995)

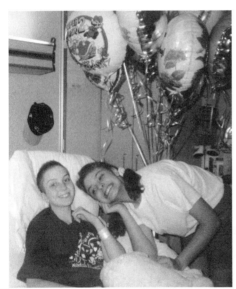

Emily and Jessica Henson, who later named her daughter after our Emily

Emily and Sebastian,
August 1995
(Used by permission of
Clemmer Photography)

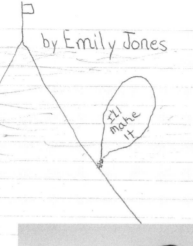

by Emily Jones

I'll make it

Emily drew this picture sometime during her two-year battle with cancer. We discovered it several months after her death. It beautifully illustrates her determination to overcome cancer.

Emily's Camp Fantastic portrait (August 1995)

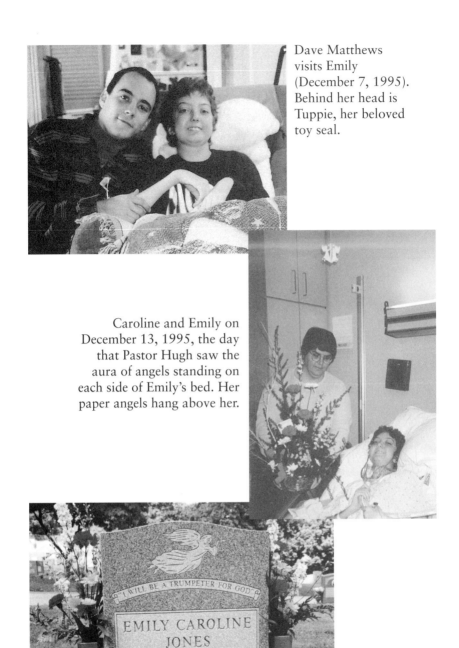

Dave Matthews visits Emily (December 7, 1995). Behind her head is Tuppie, her beloved toy seal.

Caroline and Emily on December 13, 1995, the day that Pastor Hugh saw the aura of angels standing on each side of Emily's bed. Her paper angels hang above her.

Emily's headstone, Staunton's Thornrose Cemetery

Part 2

1995

But he [Simon] replied,
   "Lord, I am ready
to go with you
to prison and to death."

                                   —Luke 22:33

Chapter 11

My birthday is coming soon. . . .
The main thing I want is a puppy.

—Emily's journal,
January 26, 1995

The protocol for continuing 5-FU indicated that Emily would have another exploratory surgery after the second round to determine if there was progression of disease. We were told that 5-FU would be stopped if Emily's cancer had spread. Surgery was scheduled for January 10. As planned, she went to school for the first week of the second semester. In fact, all of us were in school that week, and it felt good. Emily especially enjoyed time spent with her classmates; she had lots to share about her fantastic trip to the Walt Disney World Resort.

Emily saw Dr. Rice on the following Monday and was admitted for surgery on Tuesday. We were devastated but not surprised to learn that there was a clear progression of disease after a walnut-sized mass was found outside the small bowel. Dr. Dunsmore explained to Emily that cancers were very smart and could figure out ways to mutate around cancer drugs. This, she said, was what had happened with 5-FU. It was now useless in her fight against small bowel cancer. The hunt was on for another drug that could be used to wage war on Emily's tumors.

Dr. Dunsmore quickly found a new experimental drug called topotecan. We were excited that it would have fewer side effects. Either by blessing or miracle, Emily never again had mouth ulcers. She needed a pelvic MRI prior to starting the new chemotherapy, so she had one before her discharge on Friday afternoon. An additional clear progression of disease would eliminate Emily from this "second chance" trial.

Because the first round of any chemotherapy had to be done in the hospital, Emily was readmitted the following Monday. Administration of the drug took place over four days. Ten days later, she wrote about topotecan in her school journal:

> There are quite a few good things about this medicine like it only last [sic] a half an hour [administration time]. Another is I don't get sick. Plus I don't get mouth ulcers which make me unable to eat for a week and a half. One more is that it might not make me loose [sic] my hair again. I hope not. I have grown a fourth of an inch of hair which is a lot compared to nothing. I worked hard for that hair. I just got started with a new chemo. It is called Topotican [sic]. My nurses call it the tropical medicine. This medicine attacks resisting tumors. My tumors are in a way resisting tumors. They haven't spread, some have shrunk, and others are just the same. Most of my main organs are clean. That is really good. All my doctors are really excited about this new drug.

Over the next three weeks, Emily went to school regularly, missing only for several outpatient appointments and an MRI. She started her second administration of topotecan on Monday, February 6, and finished the course on Thursday. On Saturday morning, she had abdominal pain and was vomiting—well-known signs of small bowel obstruction. So off we went to the ER. Following several tests in radiology, she was sent home with a diagnosis of "intermittent blockage."

Two weeks later, I accompanied Emily to yet another clinic appointment, this time for a CT scan and ultrasound. The CT scan was first. We knew the results would not be available immediately. I was allowed to stay with her during the ultrasound. It's odd how some pictures are burned into memory. Emily was stretched out on the table, her arms behind her head, her tummy exposed. A dollop of cold jelly allowed the technician to glide the probe across the contours of her abdomen. The more the tech pushed, the more tears fell from Emily's eyes. When Emily could stand it no longer, she asked the technician to stop.

"Just a little more," was the response, and she continued to push the probe in circles and figure eights. Tears dripped from the corners of Emily's eyes until the technician was satisfied that there was sufficient information for the radiologist who would read the scan. We left the ultrasound room and returned to the PCC, where Dr. Dunsmore met us with tears streaming from her eyes.

"There was no sign of tumor on your ultrasound, Emily." We all cried and hugged. Why then, I thought to myself, was the ultrasound so painful? Nonetheless, I rejoiced in the fact that the topotecan must be working. We would learn later that the CT scan was, in fact, abnormal.

The following day, we were back in the clinic to start the third round of topotecan. Emily finished it on February 24—her fourteenth birthday. That evening, she celebrated by having friends over for pizza and cake. She enjoyed opening gifts and spending "normal" time with her friends. Her big birthday wish was that she would get a puppy. For months she had lobbied for a trip to the SPCA, where she knew a little furry critter would single her out. "Daddy, please, can I have a dog?"

The response was always the same: "No."

I thought it was a good idea, but Jerry was a hard sell. Some wishes take a little longer.

Saturday, Emily awoke with abdominal cramping and vomiting. We soon found ourselves back in the ER. More x-rays revealed that, contrary to the recent "negative" ultrasound, a partial blockage was still present. The bottom line: Not all tests are accurate. This time, Emily was admitted, but she was discharged the following Tuesday.

Fibercon and Colace were added to her regimen of drugs. We were back at the clinic on Thursday with still more vomiting, but Emily was not admitted. She did not go to school the following day due to the vomiting.

In spite of the persistent abdominal pain and vomiting, Emily continued to lobby for a dog. Jerry will tell you that he had a moment of weakness, but in truth he knew that if we were going to allow Emily to have a dog, we could wait no longer. So the next day, one high-flying fourteen-year-old and her mom made a trip to our local SPCA.

As we walked around the SPCA, every kennel we passed contained a perky, tail wagging, take-me-home-with-you dog whose paws and nose were pressed against the chain link gate. Every kennel except one, that is. "Sebastian," a stocky cocker/Lhasa Apso mix, sat quietly in his kennel. He made no effort to make eye contact and didn't seem particularly interested in the mother/daughter duo who had already strolled past his enclosure once. He had floppy ears, a blond curly coat, and a black, Chinese-looking moustache that drooped from his muzzle. He looked sad and forlorn. "INCORRIGIBLE" was printed in bold letters beside his name. "What in the world?" I wondered to myself. I was either too naïve or scared to ask.

We made two more loops of the kennel area. Both times, Emily stopped at Sebastian's cage and looked into his sad little eyes. "This is the one I want, Momma," she said at last.

"It says Sebastian is 'incorrigible,' Emily." But the choice had been made. She was already in love with Sebastian the Incorrigible. I told the attendant that we were interested in him, and she then directed us to a separate room, where we were given a few minutes to see if we could bond with the likely new member of our household. Sebastian ran from toy to toy. He may have lifted his leg on a ball—I don't remember—but based on future behavior, I suspect he did!

Before we could actually adopt Sebastian, Jerry had to agree. Emily burst into the living room as soon as we got home to tell her dad that she had a dog and that Jerry had to come back with us to the SPCA to tell them it was okay and sign some papers. The three of us went into the visitation room. Sebastian was brought back and again ran from toy to toy. Jerry agreed that he was cute and that if Emily really wanted him, we would take him home that day. We left the SPCA that early March afternoon with a cute little dog and not the first clue as to how to care for him. Neither Jerry nor I had ever owned a dog. We were in for a few surprises.

Sebastian weighed about thirty-five pounds. He had short legs and was solid. He loved to eat. I learned just how much the first night when I left a full loaf of bread on the futon in the family room. With never a thought about its vulnerability, I left it there while I went to get a load of laundry from the dryer. I returned to find a few shredded scraps of plastic but not one crumb of an entire loaf of bread. Sebastian didn't even look guilty. I was not happy, to say the least, and had second thoughts about bringing this incorrigible pooch into our household. Jerry had that "I knew this would happen" look on his face.

The next morning, I still felt as if we had made a mistake, and I told Emily that I thought we would probably have to take Sebastian back to the SPCA. She burst into tears and started yelling at me that I simply could not do that to her dog. My stomach was in knots, and who knows how high my blood pressure went, but Emily was absolutely right; I could not return her dog.

Even though he was a food guarder, who a few days later bit Bubbles's hand and drew blood over a box of chocolates she had stored under her chair, Sebastian remained a member of our family for many years. Emily had nine wonderful months with him. They were kindred spirits.

Emily's getting-to-know-you period with Sebastian lasted only two days. She was admitted to the hospital on Monday morning with an intestinal blockage and had her fourth major surgery on March 7. Because her cancer had clearly spread, the "second chance" chemo was discontinued. We were running out of options.

Following surgery, Emily was pale and listless. She was unwilling to leave the room or participate in the hospital school. Talking about Sebastian was the only thing that made her happy. Her nurse even suggested that we sneak Sebastian into her hospital room for a surprise visit. No way.

After receiving two units of blood, however, Emily perked up substantially. After another week of recovery, she was granted a four-hour Saturday daylight furlough and a nine-hour one on Sunday to visit with Auntie Ann and Lynn. She even baked cookies for them. By Sunday night, she was ready to go home, and on the next day, she was discharged after a fifteen-day admission.

Often after major surgery, Emily would be given Total Parenteral Nutrition (TPN) through her IV. This specifically formulated "food" was based on her nutritional needs. Hospital TPN was yellow and always had a brown bag placed over it on the IV pole. With her intestinal blockages becoming more severe, TPN would become important for her survival. It was not long until I was taught how to do home administration of TPN.

Susan Shipp, our primary Home I.V. Care nurse, was an excellent teacher, and I learned the process quickly. Home I.V. provided us with an apartment-sized refrigerator that we installed in our dining room. TPN, along with the tubing necessary to administer it, was soon delivered directly to our house. Home TPN was white. The number of vitamins and minerals and amount of fat were adjusted weekly based on Emily's blood work. TPN was dreadfully expensive. Twice I punctured the bag while trying to insert the tubing and had to discard the TPN in the sink. Talk about "money down the drain"!

By the end of March, Emily was complaining of back pain. Dr. Dunsmore admitted her on March 30 and requested consultations from orthopedics. The unspoken worry for us was, of course, that cancer had invaded her back. Thankfully, no cancer was detected, but there was considerable discussion about whether she had a condition that affects spinal plates and discs in the vertebrae. I don't think a final diagnosis was ever confirmed, but physical therapy was recommended. An appointment was made with a local therapist for the week after Easter.

Emily was discharged from the hospital on April 1, only to be readmitted two days later to begin the first course of Taxol and carboplatin—her third type of chemotherapy. Before she could start, she and Jerry had to sign the consent to participate in the Phase 1 study of these two drugs. Phase 1 studies come with risks, such as "uncommon or previously unknown side effects" and "life-threatening complications." Emily did not care about the risks, believing that any of these trials could hold the miracle cure she needed.

Emily remained in the hospital for seven days. After discharge, she was feeling remarkably good, complaining only of intermittent headaches and only occasionally throwing up. She also had a slight tingling in her fingers, which was a rare but documented side effect of the new chemo. Regular doses of morphine gave her excellent pain relief. In addition, she took an antinausea drug and a precautionary antibiotic.

With Emily feeling good after the first round of Taxol and carboplatin, Jerry felt strongly that we needed to go away during our school system's spring break, which coincided with Easter. The girls immediately decided upon Charleston, South Carolina, where we had been previously during other spring breaks. This trip would be our third. Bubbles decided to come with us, too. She made the right choice.

A four-day trip took a huge amount of planning. Emily's doctors gave their blessings, but Dr. Dunsmore also contacted the hospital at the University of South Carolina to give them information on Emily, since we would be in their area. We were given a phone number to use in case she should need medical attention. Because her blood counts were low following chemotherapy, we were given precautions for the beach.

Taking Sebastian on vacation with us was never an option, so we had to find doggie care for him. Fortunately, our good friends Koressa and Joe Malcolm had offered to keep Sebastian whenever necessary. They lived in rural Highland County, about forty-five miles west of Staunton. Joe had a veterinary practice there, and Koressa was a school psychologist in Augusta County. Knowing that Joe would treat Sebastian if he were injured or became sick eased our concerns over leaving him for the first time. Granted, Sebastian had been a member of our household only a month, but he had endeared himself to us just as he had to Emily.

Highland County borders West Virginia. It is often called "Little Switzerland." The road there from Staunton is two lanes and has plenty of hairpin turns. Koressa met Sebastian and me in Staunton on the Thursday before Easter. She had installed a dog crate in the back of her car, and Sebastian jumped right in. Who knew that he would get car sick on the ride to Highland?

Malcolm Doggie Camp was wonderful for Sebastian. He wasn't confined in a kennel, and he simply adored the Malcolms' two children, not to mention their pets and farm animals. He loved to chase Koressa's chickens. She rather liked this, since Sebastian kept the hens from scratching in her garden. Over the eleven years that

Sebastian lived with us, he attended Malcolm Doggie Camp many times. It was his second home.

Instead of staying right in Charleston, Jerry booked rooms for us at a resort on Kiawah Island, southeast of the city. The beach there is heavenly—wide and inviting. I made arrangements with Home I.V. for early delivery of enough TPN and morphine and other medications to last five days. Jerry contacted the hotel to make sure a refrigerator would be available and to tell them we were bringing a huge number of medications with us. He did not want the hotel staff to think we were drug dealers!

Home I.V. delivered two large coolers to store the refrigerated supplies during the drive to South Carolina. With excellent pain management, Emily was in great shape and eager for this vacation. In spite of the fact that most of her nutrition came from TPN, she was hungry for seafood and tempting desserts.

We left early on Good Friday. Every inch of extra space in the van was needed to store luggage for five, Bubbles's wheelchair, the two giant coolers, and five people. Nine or so hours later, we checked into our beautiful rooms on Kiawah Island. The air was thick and warm. We were surrounded by lush, tropical green and an abundance of palm trees—truly a little bit of paradise.

Kiawah Island is a golf resort, but there were plenty of activities for nongolfers like us. Ann and Emily rented bikes to explore the island's crisscrossed, paved paths. The beach had firmly packed sand, as well, so bikers could easily ride along the shoreline. Ann and Emily enjoyed some splendid rides together, exploring trails and pedaling on the packed sand. One of Jerry's

> Be exalted, O God,
>   above the heavens,
> and let your glory be
>   over all the earth.
>
> —Psalm 108:5

favorite pictures of the girls was taken as they pushed their bikes across the wooden walkway leading to the beach, a cool wind blowing from the ocean. Except for the backpack containing Emily's morphine pump, there is not one hint of Emily's illness in that picture.

As we had done on previous trips to Charleston, we went to Trinity United Methodist Church on Meeting Street to worship on Easter Sunday morning. Bubbles marveled at the church's magnificent interior as well as the glorious music provided by the organist and choir. It felt so good to celebrate the risen Lord together in that splendid place. The next Easter would be so very different.

Following church, we had lunch at Tommy Condon's Irish Pub, another of our favorite Charleston spots. We had planned to sightsee afterward, until I realized that I had left Emily's medication at the hotel. Jerry was justifiably irritated with me, but there was nothing to do except return to Kiawah Island. Things have a way of working out, though. That afternoon, Emily invited Jerry to join her on a bike ride. Together they pedaled Kiawah's bike paths for maybe an hour. Jerry remembers the afternoon with a particular sweetness.

The date of Easter is determined by the first full moon after the spring equinox. Sometimes the full moon, known in Christianity as an Ecclesiastical Full Moon, falls exactly on Easter and other times not. Easter Sunday 1995 had an Ecclesiastical Full Moon, huge, pink, and spectacular as it edged slowly above the Atlantic horizon. In the cool of Easter evening, the girls and I stood on the wooden walk between the dunes and beach to watch it rise, awed by its majesty. A wonderful ocean breeze kissed our skin. Oh, if only I could have frozen that moment forever.

Eating out was always a treat when we were on vacation. No one loved dressing up and going out to a fancy restaurant more than Emily. When she was seven years old, we spent one night at Mountain Lake, a well-known resort located in western Virginia within a few miles of Newport, the village where the Jones-Hutchison family reunions were held.

Ann and Emily had been especially excited about spending a night at Mountain Lake, since it was the location for many scenes from the unexpected motion picture hit *Dirty Dancing*. In the movie, Frances "Baby" Houseman (Jennifer Grey) and her family are at a holiday camp (Mountain Lake). Baby meets and falls for the camp's dance instructor, Johnny Castle (Patrick Swayze). Being on the set of a successful movie was extremely appealing to our girls. We didn't stay in the resort hotel but in one of the cabins, just like Baby and her family. It was truly fun.

In the film, guests staying at the resort dressed for dinner. The real-life resort followed the same protocol. Emily "Clothes Horse" Jones selected a special outfit to wear—a black-and-white plaid, drop-waist dress with a hip-hugging sash and bow. The dress bore a distinct resemblance to Pollyanna's fancy dresses that had been bought by her Aunt Polly. Emily was skinny, and the dress looked cute on her. To complete her outfit, she wore black patent-leather shoes with white socks and had white gloves on her hands.

Mountain Lake's dining room was located in the lower level of the stone hotel, and guests staying in cabins had a fair distance to walk, which was perfect for Emily, who had mastered a "Pollyanna hip swing" so that she could sashay just like the actress Hayley Mills. I can see Emily still, a prissy little doll absorbed in an innocent world.

Emily had a knack for doing or saying unexpected things. On a previous trip to Charleston, she embarrassed the daylights out of Jerry. We were staying in a nice downtown hotel, and Jerry had made dinner reservations for us in the hotel restaurant. When we arrived, many of the tables were already filled with quietly talking, well-dressed families and couples. As the maître d' led us to our table, without warning Emily let out a loud belch. Both girls started giggling uncontrollably. I know it was rude, but I laughed, too. It was funny. Jerry failed to see the humor.

On another occasion, we were riding in the car when Emily did or said something that resulted in a scolding from her dad. No sooner were the stern words out of his mouth than she fired right back, "I'm scared. Look, I'm shaking!" (a quote from *Flight of the Navigator*). It is true that Emily should not have talked back to her dad, but her spontaneity and dry humor absolutely cracked us up. There was no way anyone could stay mad at Emily for long. I miss her humor. So does Jerry.

Dining on Kiawah Island can be a first-class experience. With Emily's love of eating and her relative health following the first cycle of Taxol and carboplatin, Jerry was determined that meals on this vacation would be memorable. They were, and in ways that he had not exactly expected.

Jasmine Porch, which was located on the island, was a gorgeous place with—you guessed it—a huge porch stretching across the front overlooking the inlet. Bubbles was in her wheelchair, and rather than go to the back where a ramp was located, she used the handrail to help her up the steps so that she could ride in through the front door. We enjoyed a delicious seafood dinner while seated at a lovely table in a swank restaurant with plenty of ambiance and spectacular views. The dining experience should have ended there, but it didn't. The most unforgettable part of the evening came with Bubbles's wheelchair exit.

A twilight sky and dim lighting on the restaurant's front steps meant it was safer for Bubbles to leave in her wheelchair via the exit ramp. The ramp, however, was accessible only through the kitchen. So our waitress directed Jerry and Bubbles in that direction, while I took the girls out the main entrance. We met at the back entrance, where we found Jerry doubled over in hysterics.

According to Jerry, the kitchen staff had stopped everything as he and Bubbles cruised through on their way to the ramp. Bubbles, smiling and expressing her appreciation for their culinary talents, used her "royal" *cheerio* wave to say adieu to the chefs, who nodded and waved in return. As soon as the two of them exited the back door onto the ramp, Jerry found himself without traction and in an uncontrolled slide to the parking lot. Gripping the wheelchair handles, Jerry leaned over Bubbles's shoulder and yelled, "Hold on, we're going for a ride!"

Apparently, there had been a thin layer of grease on the ramp, which was used far more as a path to the dumpster than as a wheelchair exit. They slid to the bottom and out into the parking lot. To this day, Jerry can't tell that story with a straight face.

Turtle Point Restaurant, where we ate the next night, was located on the far end of the island. For some reason, we had to wait an unusually long time for our table. We were eventually seated at a round table with padded seats that went halfway around it. We had a wonderful waitress who apologized profusely for our seating delay. Emily ordered a lavish meal but could do no more than pick at it. Her eyes lit up with anticipation when our waitress brought "on the house," melt-in-your-mouth raspberry cheesecake for each of us. What a conclusion to a fantastic meal! Emily didn't eat all that was placed before her, but she loved trying.

Emily did extremely well on our trip to Kiawah. She did everything she wanted, ate as much as she could, and enjoyed her family, especially time spent with Ann. On Tuesday morning, we packed the car and drove home. Our last vacation as a family of five had come to an end.

Chapter 12

Hope is the armrest that holds
us cancer kids up every day.

—from Emily's speech,
Adolescent Quilting Show,
June 29, 1995

The day after we returned from Kiawah Island, Emily went to her appointment with the physical therapist to learn exercises that would help alleviate her back pain. She stopped going after several sessions, however, since she could not do the exercises with enough consistency to gain substantial benefit. At least the foam pillow that the therapist gave her to support the small of her back did provide some relief.

By late April, spring and high school prom time had arrived in the Shenandoah Valley. Emily went to school as she was able and for clinic visits as scheduled. She got TPN twelve hours out of every day. Emily shared in Ann's excitement over her date with Andy to Buffalo Gap High School's prom, which would be the last Saturday in April. I enjoyed spending time with Ann shopping for her dress. She decided upon a lovely royal-blue, figure-hugging dress that looked simply stunning on her. We still chuckle that she ate practically nothing but rice for two weeks before the dance to ensure the dress's perfect fit on prom night.

The day of the prom was beautiful that year. Andy arrived in the late afternoon to take Ann out to dinner before the dance. The nice thing about Ann and Andy was that they were good friends in addition to a dating couple. They knew how to have fun together. After spending a few minutes chatting with Emily, off they went, ready to eat, then dance away the night with their friends. I wish I could have sent Emily to that prom, hairless trendsetter in her own stunning gown and jewelry. I had so many wishes and no time to see them through.

A CT scan done on May 1 showed no new nodes or tumors in Emily's abdomen. This was fantastic news. Auntie Ann came for a quick visit, and we were almost giddy with the good report. But in just over a week, Emily was back in the hospital with abdominal pain and vomiting. Still, radiology could find no evidence of small bowel obstruction. She was discharged on Mother's Day. We desperately wanted to believe that all was well.

Some weeks earlier, Theresa Andrews had approached Emily about attending Camp Fantastic, a camp for children with cancer. It was held annually at the 4-H Educational Center in Front Royal, Virginia. This medically tailored program promised normal camping activities, such as boating, a talent show, and traditional arts and crafts. Emily was definitely interested and expected me to pursue the application. I never did, mainly because I didn't think she would be well enough to attend a week-long camp in late August.

I do not recall exactly how the topic arose, but during a clinic appointment in late May, someone—possibly Theresa—asked Emily about attending the camp. Emily turned to me and bluntly asked if I had completed the application. I had to confess the truth. She did not hold back her anger and blasted me full force in the clinic hallway. Red embarrassment flushed my face as I turned to

Theresa and pleaded with her to get a spot for Emily in this camp. I promised that even if I had to drive Emily to and from Front Royal daily, I would gladly do it.

Camp Fantastic '95 had space for seventy-five to eighty-five campers. Most were accepted on a first-come, first-served basis. We were well past the May 1 application deadline, but Theresa promised to call the camp director immediately to see if something could be worked out. Indeed, the camp was full, but one camper had recently backed out, freeing a single spot. Emily was in, and I felt the greatest sense of relief. We submitted her application on June 2.

Excellent pain management made it possible for Emily to live an amazingly full life during that spring. She especially anticipated the hospital's Family Day, which would be held on a Saturday in late May at Camp Holiday Trails, located on a beautiful tract of land just south of Charlottesville. The day was warm and sunny, and lots of cancer patients and their families came.

Emily had become good friends with several of the other teenage girls, and she especially enjoyed being with them in a camp setting with two must-haves: food and entertainment. Lots of the medical staff came, too. Pat Cobb, Emily's beloved PCC nurse; Janet Stewart, our faithful nurse clinician; and Theresa Andrews were there.

Dr. De Alarcon came with his daughter, who was a year or two younger than Emily. She and Ann and Emily went canoeing together on the lake. I snapped several pictures of the three girls in their canoe. Emily didn't know the first thing about paddling, but she had a good time. Away from the hospital, children didn't seem so sick and families didn't seem so traumatized. The day was a huge success, and we returned home with some really good memories.

Early the next week, Emily went to a regularly scheduled outpatient appointment. During a down time in the exam room, she was visited by a child psychologist, who offered to meet with and counsel her. Emily emphatically refused her services. That same day, Dr. Dunsmore wrote in her update letter to Dr. Massey, "My assessment is that Emily is doing really well after her second cycle of Taxol and carboplatin." She was doing so well that Dr. Dunsmore wanted her to decrease the amount of morphine she was getting. Hope was in the air.

Before the week was out, though, Emily was back in the ER with vomiting and abdominal pain. She was admitted, and an NG tube was inserted. More x-rays showed "no evidence for obstruction or perforation." However, the next day x-rays were made with the NG tube clamped. They showed dilation of small bowel loops. The note in Emily's chart said they were "worrisome for partial small bowel obstruction." Once again we were on the roller coaster, and more surgery was a very likely possibility. In spite of a probable obstruction, her NG tube was removed on May 30, and she was given an afternoon furlough.

We were back at the hospital the next day. The CT scan conducted on June 1 showed her liver, spleen, pancreas, and kidneys to be "unremarkable," while a previously identified cervical mass was thought to be slightly larger. With the x-rays and scans completed, we were given a Saturday/Sunday furlough. You would think we would have stayed as far away from the hospital as possible, but the Children's Miracle Network Telethon was the same weekend, and Emily was not about to miss the glitz and glitter of this annual event.

She and I returned to the seventh floor that evening. Emily wore a cute little skirt, a sleeveless top, and her black velvet hat, since Taxol and carboplatin had left her completely hairless and with only an assortment of freckles on her face. She looked amazing with a little red lipstick and a perky smile on her lips.

Emily made two appearances on the 1995 telethon: one Saturday night and the other late on Sunday afternoon. It was during that second appearance that Robert Van Winkle again conducted a short personal interview with her on camera. He mentioned that he'd heard she was going to have surgery the following day. She corrected him and said the surgery would be either Tuesday or Thursday. He then asked her about her many hospitalizations. "Is that right?" he exclaimed when Emily announced that, to date, she had been an inpatient for one hundred days. I think he was genuinely surprised.

We didn't leave the hospital Sunday night until the telethon was over, and we were back the next morning. Emily was admitted from the clinic to the seventh floor. Later that day, a fluoroscopic exam indicated the likely spread of cancer in the small and large bowel. She was scheduled for surgery to address the bowel obstruction. Also, a gastrostomy tube (G-tube) was to be placed in her abdomen to relieve stress on her poorly functioning bowel and to allow her to eat without passing food into the bowel. TPN would provide 100 percent of her nutrition from this point forward.

Dr. McGahren performed Emily's surgery, which, in addition to everything else, included exploration to determine how far her cancer had spread. The news was not good. Emily's cancer was now widespread throughout her lower torso, with new tumors forming in the abdominal area. Dr. McGahren told Jerry and me privately that if the cancer ruptured a major vessel or artery (and that was a very real possibility), she would not survive. Death would be quick. I felt sick to my stomach, extremely frightened, and totally helpless.

As expected, Emily was really sore the day after her surgery. In addition to morphine, pain patches were used to help control her discomfort. Jerry and I opted not to share what we had learned from Dr. McGahren with her. Later in the afternoon, our pastor stopped by for a visit. While he was there, Dr. Dunsmore entered the room. She spent a few minutes chatting about the surgery and the benefits of the G-tube. Then she got quite serious and spoke directly to Emily, explaining in a compassionate manner that the cancer had spread, and the Taxol/carboplatin trial would not continue.

I don't think Emily was surprised. Then Dr. Dunsmore told her that not only would this trial end, but there were no more experimental drugs available for her to try. In a quiet voice, Dr. Dunsmore told Emily that she had about six months to live and that she should go home to decide how she wanted to use the time left to her.

Jerry and I sobbed, but not Emily. With not so much as a quiver in her voice she pointed her "ET" finger (the one with the oxygen meter attached) at Dr. Dunsmore and demanded that a chemo be found for her immediately, because God had told her in her heart that she would be healed. Dr. Dunsmore responded that Emily might have to go to St. Jude's.

"I'll go tomorrow!" she said. "Just find me a chemo."

Dr. Dunsmore said that she would see what she could do. Three days later, Emily concluded a rather long entry in her journal with these words:

> I saved something for last. Dr. Dunsmore said on Friday that she had done everything she could do here. All she could do was call St. Judds [sic] or National Cancer Institute. She also said anything that they had probably had less than a 4% chance of curing me. I said call St. Judds. She said I probably only had months. She also said if I did more chemo those few months would be miserable.
>
> Well today she said she has two chemos for me at St. Judds. They are stage ones which mean we don't know sideaffects [sic] or toxicicies [sic]. I said well go for it. She said to think about it. They didn't even have names. I said find out more. I have to go.
>
> June 12, 1995

Emily absolutely refused to be defeated or even acknowledge that she might die, as an entry in her diary that month made clear:

> Well I also found out today that some untrue rumurs [sic] are being spread around like my liver is failing and I am dying. Please!

This child had unshakable faith in complete healing. There was no doubt in her belief system. She inspired and astounded me and at the same time made me ashamed that my own faith was clouded by what my eyes saw and my ears heard.

Emily bounced back from her exploratory surgery and G-tube placement amazingly well. Soon she was up and walking slow laps around 7 Central. A few days later, she was sailing around her hospital track. She was so adorable in her big yellow Mickey Mouse bedroom slippers that I simply had to video her exercise routine.

On her fifth loop around the 7 Central nurses' station, Bill, a fun-loving nurse, held up his hand to halt her just like a policeman directing traffic. Emily stopped, and Bill motioned for a nurse to cross from the nurses' station into a patient's room. If Bill had had a whistle, he would have blown it as he signaled Emily to resume her walk. When she arrived back at her own room a minute or so later, she waved to the camera and ducked inside, announcing that she was ready for a rest. It was amazing that just seven days had passed since her surgery.

Later that same evening, Emily, Jerry, and Theresa Andrews met with a group of medical students. Emily had been invited to talk with these doctors-to-be about bedside manners. In her classic, straightforward style, she told them that they needed to have empathy for their patients, be gentle, and listen well to what their patients said, even if they were just kids. I heard later that she'd made a remarkable impression on those men and women. I trust they are better doctors because of her.

Emily also endeared herself to a number of the pediatric residents. One group gave her a UVA Pediatrics sweatshirt, which she wore often and with great pride. In fact, she had it on when she did her laps around the nurses' station.

One of Emily's favorites was resident Judy Bernhard, who regularly visited her. Judy was aware of the most recent surgery and dropped by for a chat, bringing Emily a purple t-shirt with stars and a moon on it. Years later, as I read Emily's diary, I found a specific reference to Judy's visit. Emily wrote that they talked about "faith and other stuff." She also wrote, "I love her so much." How wonderful that she had such a special friend and confidant.

Before Emily could be discharged from the hospital, she and I had to learn basic G-tube care. Clamping it to administer medications and keeping the wound area clean seemed simple enough, but I was secretly terrified that it would somehow dislodge, deflate, or—horrors—come out. Emily, however, was completely confident in replacing the catheter if it came out. The nurses assured me that if it did, it would not pose a medical emergency. Fortunately, nothing ever happened to it.

Emily loved demonstrating her G-tube to friends and family. One evening while Emily was still in the hospital, Katie Propst came for a visit. The two of them were sharing the hospital bed when Katie decided to video Emily eating a candy bar so that everyone could see the chewed remains float out of the tube seconds later. Emily happily showed off where the catheter entered her body and also how she would inflate it with exactly five cc's of air if it were to come out and need to be reinserted. Katie joked the whole time, making all sorts of comments about her friend's latest medical device.

Emily remained hospitalized for the next five days. She had developed a cough, but x-rays revealed that she did not have pneumonia. Dr. Dunsmore met with Jerry and me on Thursday to discuss Emily's anticipated discharge the next day. Even though Emily was walking well and managing the G-tube and TPN, she was extremely nervous about being discharged from the hospital. In fact, she had confessed to her night nurse that she was terrified that her pain could not be controlled outside the hospital environment. Nurse Katherine was so concerned about Emily's mental state that she made a note in the chart.

Just before Emily's discharge, Dr. Dunsmore again reiterated with us that the chances of finding a new chemotherapy for her were almost nil, and, even if one *was* found, the side effects would likely be very hard for Emily to manage. We knew this was true. I secretly hoped Emily could somehow bypass the agony of another experimental chemo. All of us knew that now was the time for our miracle.

After talking with Emily, we decided that rather than go home, we would get a room at a nearby hotel for the weekend. She would be more confident knowing she was only ten minutes from the ER. It is quite possible that the dosage of medication was not fully controlling her pain, since she was so reluctant to go far from the hospital. She'd had a morphine pump for several months, and until recently, it had provided adequate pain management. Our hope was that with the addition of pain patches, Emily would be able to function fairly normally.

She tried so hard to keep a chin-up attitude, but often the look on her face or her slumped posture told a different story. We were

> Heal me, O Lord, and I will be healed;
>
> save me and I will be saved,
>
> for you are the one I praise.
>
> —*Jeremiah 17:14*

truly grateful that her doctors were always aggressive about pain management.

Emily was discharged to our care on Friday, June 17. Auntie Ann, Lynn, and Bubbles joined us at the Boar's Head Inn, which is located just outside the city limits, to be a part of her "welcome home" party. I made a short video of our little "homecoming." We ordered take-out from Tiffany's, a popular local seafood restaurant, and tried to have a normal dinner in the comfort of our hotel room.

Emily didn't smile much and wasn't in a very talkative mood. She ate little and spent much of the time curled up on the bed. She did, however, make it through the weekend without any trips to the ER. We came home on Father's Day. Within another week or so, she was feeling better. The G-tube was working well, and we were succeeding with pain management.

Because Emily would be continuously tethered to a drainage bag, she decided to conceal it in a small cloth pouch with straps so that she could carry it over her arm like a purse. Most people were unaware of her G-tube or morphine pump, which she also stored in the purse. Of course, all of her nutrition came from TPN. The beauty of the G-tube was that she could still derive pleasure from eating despite the fact that her bowel was barely functioning.

By the third week in June, Emily was doing much better and our lives were amazingly normal. Ann went to Virginia Girls' State, returning home on the twenty-third. The next day, Jerry's family came for a visit. Andy was over visiting Ann, too. The afternoon was hot, so we decided to have a backyard water-balloon battle.

Emily and the others paired off to toss the water-filled balloons. PawPaw Elmer was the first one to get soaked. We laughed until we cried that afternoon. Emily's partner was Andy. He made sure she could catch balloons tossed at her. I made a video of the balloon toss; it's one of the ones that I love to review, as it is filled with laughter and fun.

Sometime before school had ended for the year, I had received a note from Karen Hays, my teacher friend, inviting us to join her at the Richmond Christian Center to hear Kenneth Hagen, a well-known evangelist. Karen wrote that "there is a powerful anointing on his life and there will be hundreds of people there to hear him. The collective anointing of so many believers in one place is what is needed for Emily's healing."

She encouraged us to pray and "do as the Holy Spirit leads and guides you to do." I did pray about that conference, and I went. It was uplifting and powerful, just as Karen had promised. I remember that Kenneth Hagen spoke boldly about the Holy Spirit. It was good for me to hear his message.

An even stronger message came to me through Karen's sister. Sharon had attended an evangelical conference in Richmond at around the same time. After the leader had finished his talk, he'd stopped and said that the Lord told him someone in the audience was praying for a Caroline. He asked that she come forward, but no one did. Then he said that the Lord said to tell her that she (Caroline) would have her victory.

Sharon thought to herself that she was not praying for anyone named Caroline. The Lord spoke to Sharon and said that, indeed, she was praying for someone by that name, that Emily's mother was named Caroline. Now, I might not have been the Caroline referenced by the speaker, but I believed that I was. I stood on that message, claimed *my* victory, and awaited *my* miracle. Daily we read the scripture from Exodus 15:26: ". . . for I am the Lord, who heals you." I usually rephrased it to say, "I am the God who heals Emily."

The month would draw to a close with Emily becoming one of several adolescent patient stars during a Grand Rounds presentation at the Camp Heart Center at UVA Hospital on June 29. The Hospital Education Program had been invited to make a presentation about the Adolescent Quilting Project. Emily was asked to talk about her most recent quilt, which she had named "Pandora's Box," and about a song she had written as a participant in the CMC/HEP Creative Writing Workshop for Teens conducted by David Kleiner and funded by a grant from the Virginia Department of Education.

Emily was thrilled to be asked and eager to tell her story before a large group of hospital staff. Many of her doctors were in attendance. She also had a large cheering section of her own family and friends, including Bubbles, Bubbles's brother and sister-in-law from South Carolina, a friend from England, Emily's friend Katie, our neighbor Margie, Ann, two "tween" girls Ann was caring for over the summer while their parents worked, and Emily's extremely proud parents.

Marta Gilliam hosted the event. She talked about the power of art and music to transform a teenager's hospital stay from dull and frightening to energized and exciting. Teenage patients walked to the podium one by one to tell the stories behind their quilts and original songs. Local musicians were on hand to perform several of the songs as well.

When Emily's turn came, she approached the podium with her little G-tube purse over her left arm as usual. She wore her Mickey Mouse baseball cap on her mostly hairless head. Here is the script she wrote for herself:

> Hi! My name is Emily Jones. I'm 14 years old, and I have adenocarcinoma of the small bowel. Last October I started working on my second quilt called Pandora's Box. I got the idea because this year I took Latin, and Marta liked the idea

of doing mythological quilts. Marta started naming stories and said "Pandora," and I said, "I'm studying Pandora in school and I want to do that one." So from then on I started working on my quilt.

I looked up the story in some books and then began to piece things together in my mind. I just started taking pieces of fabric to make her skirt. Her profile is mine. If you look closely, you'll see the resemblance. [Emily turned sideways so the audience could see her profile. Everyone burst out laughing.]

The hair isn't mine! [More laughter.] This quilt means a lot to me, though, because, as you know, cancer kids have to have *hope*, and that's what Pandora had left in her box. Hope is the armrest that holds us cancer kids up every day. Making this quilt has been wonderful for me. I'd like to say a special thank you to the ladies who finished it for me.

Another great activity I've gotten to do while I'm in the hospital is write a song. I've never written a song in my life, but with David Kleiner encouraging me, it was like I'd written 20 million. I just started saying things and by the time I was done, I had a song—or at least the lyrics. I should really thank Marta for finding David. Without both of them, between these two activities, I wouldn't have anything.

When Emily finished, the audience erupted in loud applause. I'd never been prouder of her. Immediately after she stepped down from the podium, Marta introduced David Kleiner, who described how, over the weeks that he had worked with Emily, she had not only written the lyrics but composed the tune. People laughed when he said that he had asked to change just one chord. He then sang Emily's song while playing it on his guitar. "Cancer for Christmas" was beautiful, poignant, and left many in the audience in tears.

Two weeks later, Emily received a lovely letter from Dr. Sharon Hostler, the McLemore Birdsong Professor of Pediatrics at UVA Hospital. The letter is a treasure, a wonderful verification of Emily's strength and character. This accomplished doctor wrote:

Your sensitive and poised comments during the quilting gala about your own prolonged hospitalization were most meaningful to me as I sat in the audience with my medical students. What an exceptional person you are! Thank you for sharing with us. My students are still talking about your magnificent presentation.

Back in mid-January, Emily had received a letter from the editor of *Girls' Life*, asking for an update on her condition. In addition to the hundreds of letters that Emily had personally received during the months since her article was published, many more girls had written the magazine asking about Emily's progress. Emily, who had a strong penchant for procrastination, had not yet complied with the editor's request. After she got home from the hospital that day, however, she asked for a copy of her remarks and included a very personal letter, part of which said:

Please tell everyone no matter how bad things get you always have hope. I would like you to also tell people that I am very sorry I haven't written back but I have been ill and busy. . . . Now about me: I finished school. I will be starting 9th grade in August. I had a quilt show today where I had to speak and this guy sang my song "Cancer for Christmas." I got a lot of comments. It was fun.

I have also been doing a lot of shopping. I am really trying to get out and get my mind off things. I have also put my faith in God. I have decided that God is going to heal me and that is it. I think now that God is everything to me. I fully believe God is going to heal me. I keep my spirits up and believe I am going to be healed and that's how I get by every day. Well, that's my battle plan: God, believing I am healed, and keeping my spirits high!

Love,
Emily

A follow-up article on Emily's condition was published in the August/September 1995 issue of *Girls' Life*.

June had taken our family from the lowest low to the highest high. At the close of the month, Emily looked so good—even healthy. She was active, happy, and full of Spirit-driven optimism. She could hardly wait for July to arrive—Kadee Boone was coming from Georgia, and Emily had some big plans for herself and her two best friends, Katie and Kadee.

Chapter 13

These are tears of joy.

—Emily to an elementary school student,
October 13, 1995

July 4 fell on a Tuesday in 1995. Unlike so many years before, Emily mostly watched as Ann and our friends Monika, Michele, Oak, and Diane Huffer decorated the front porch and fence with balloons and streamers. Later in the day, our back porch was filled with grandparents, aunts and uncles, cousins, and neighbors. Katie and Andy had also come over. Emily's uncle, Sam Canode, brought a small arsenal of firecrackers to set off in the yard. Emily had decorated another flag cake using strawberries and blueberries. The day was hot, and strawberry juice ran all over the white icing.

Festivities at Gypsy Hill Park were lower key that year, since the Statler Brothers were no longer performing. However, the parade went on as usual. Local music groups played throughout the day, church and civic groups ran their food booths, and in the evening a recognized country music star performed until time for the fireworks. Emily, Katie, and Jerry lit sparklers on the patio ahead of the big fireworks display. By the time all the festivities were over, Emily was wiped out. I'm grateful she was well enough to celebrate America's birthday one last time.

The following Sunday, Kadee arrived for a four-day visit. She and Emily spent hours talking and sharing teenage secrets. Kadee accompanied Emily to her clinic appointment on Monday, and I followed along, making a video as Emily gave her friend a private tour of the seventh floor and the Primary Care Center.

On another afternoon, the girls and Katie Propst went swimming in a friend's pool. Emily was very protective of her port and made sure it stayed dry, but she still enjoyed floating in an inner tube. Although being in the pool made it even clearer that she was the color of a blanched almond, at least her hair was growing back, since she was no longer receiving chemotherapy. She periodically ran her slender fingers across the top of her head, just as I remember my father doing first thing in the morning. The three girls bobbed contentedly around in the water until it was time to go home.

Jerry and I also took Emily and Kadee to a musical at Lime Kiln, a beautiful outdoor theater located in Lexington, south of Staunton. *Stonewall Country,* a play written by Don Baker with music by local musicians Robin and Linda Williams, told the story of General "Stonewall" Jackson, right-hand man to General Robert E. Lee. Emily and Kadee sat in the front row, clapping and laughing along with the audience to the catchy yet meaningful songs. No one would ever have guessed that Emily's life clock was ticking down.

Kadee went home on Wednesday. I don't remember if Kadee and Emily shed tears as they hugged one another goodbye. Looking back, I wonder if either of them thought that this visit would be their last. It was. Five months later, Kadee and her parents would travel nearly all night to get to Staunton for Emily's funeral. I remember Kadee's soft weeping as she and her dad stood beside Emily in her casket and grieved the loss of her beloved friend. I thought my heart would break.

Kadee's mom is a gifted musician and a woman of deep faith. Shortly before Kadee came to Virginia for her visit, her mom wrote the lyrics to a song. Randi dedicated it to Emily.

I Give My All to You

When I hear your voice inside
There is where I can abide.
You are there to protect me
You are there to guide.
You lead me through gentle waters
You see me through the worst of times.
The cross You carried for me
You forgave me at Calvary.
With this heart I will love You.
With this song I will worship and praise.
With this life there'll be heavenly grandeur,
Doing my Father's will.
Forever You'll be,
Living in me.
I give my all to You.

In my soul it's peace I find
Your loving words can soothe my restless mind.
There is comfort in Your presence
I can leave all fears behind.
You give me strength in my weakness.
Your angels bring showers of heavenly light.
There is no darkness for me
My Savior's blood was shed to set me free.
With this heart I will love You.
With this song I will worship and praise.

1995

With this life there'll be heavenly grandeur,

Doing my Father's will.

Forever you'll be,

Living in me.

I give my all to You.

Forever You'll be,

Living in me.

I give my all to You.

— *Randi Boone, July 5, 1995*

At our July 10 appointment, Dr. Dunsmore expressed pleasure that Emily was "clinically stable." She planned for Emily to return to the clinic in one week to start a palliative chemotherapy. As with any new chemotherapy, Emily would be admitted to the hospital for the first course. She was excited and ready.

A week later, we were back at the hospital, not to begin the new chemotherapy but to get the results of more blood work. Several days earlier, Emily had experienced mild nausea as well as problems with decreased, greenish output from her G-tube. Her skin and the whites of her eyes had a yellowish tint and her legs were puffy. A short while later, we learned that her liver was not fully functioning. She also had obstructive symptoms. Dr. Dunsmore had us wait in the PCC while she discussed Emily's situation with pediatric surgeons and with pediatric oncologists at the National Institutes of Health (NIH). Jerry and I were suspicious that Emily would not be able to start a new chemotherapy.

Normally we would have been happy to avoid an admission, but the news delivered by Dr. Dunsmore was not good. Later that day, she would write to Dr. Massey, our family doctor in Staunton to whom monthly reports were sent, "I am very sorry for the turn of events for Emily and hope that we can maintain some quality of life for whatever time she has left."

Emily certainly understood the impact of the news from Dr. Dunsmore. Frankly, I don't think she was very surprised by it. Although she tried to appear outwardly upbeat and positive, she was keenly aware of how she felt on the inside. She was seriously let down that she wouldn't be admitted to the hospital, however, because she'd had her heart set on attending a special event on the seventh floor.

The Dave Matthews Band, which had formed in Charlottesville, was rapidly rising to fame. They had graciously agreed to hold a "signing party" for patients and their families. It was to be quite a gala event. Fortunately, someone let Nancy Artis, the HEP director, know that Emily was in the clinic and that she really wanted to meet this group. Before long the Dave Matthews Band descended upon her clinic room.

Emily never left the clinic room's vinyl chair. Rather, each of the band members came to her, introduced himself, and chatted briefly with her. Someone took a Polaroid picture of the group surrounding her. Dave drew a picture on the card to which the snapshot was attached before settling beside her for a short, one-on-one conversation. All of them signed posters, CDs, and tapes for Emily and Ann, who was away at a church event. The band stayed perhaps fifteen or twenty minutes, then they were gone. In those few minutes, a most remarkable friendship was formed.

After consulting with pediatric surgeons and the NIH, Dr. Dunsmore shared with Emily, Jerry, and me that she would be unable to start the palliative chemotherapy. She did say that a biliary ultrasound had been recommended. We decided that we would rather go home and return the following day for that test. Dr. Dunsmore mentioned that Emily might benefit from a urinary catheter, but she refused. Jerry and I were instructed on emergency situations that might arise that would require a call or a return to the hospital.

The next morning, we were back in the clinic for the ultrasound. While we waited for the results, the HEP director came to see us. She told Emily that Dave Matthews was quite taken with her and had invited her to be his guest at a concert in Richmond the following week. He would provide her with a backstage pass. He also asked for her phone number (which he later wrote on his shoe for safe-keeping). Emily beamed, as would any teenager who had just been singled out by a rock star. Jerry thought we could easily combine the concert with a planned overnight trip to take Ann, who at the age of sixteen had already begun thinking about her post–high school education, to visit the campus of a prospective college in Fredericksburg.

After Nancy Artis left, we met with Dr. Dunsmore, who told us that Emily had an obstruction in the bile duct and would be admitted two days later for placement of a stent. That morning found us admitted to the seventh floor, not for palliative chemotherapy, but for a procedure which would, it was hoped, help her liver rid itself of bile.

While Emily was in recovery, the gastroenterologist showed me an image of Emily's liver. I saw a large, gray, mostly round shape with something that looked like a stalk of broccoli at the bottom. He said in a healthy liver, I would see something more like a large tree than a single stalk of broccoli, and there would be no gray spaces. So there it was; Emily's liver was barely functioning.

After successful placement of the stent and a brief hospital stay, Emily was discharged. The following day, we returned to the clinic for an abdominal x-ray and labs. The Dave Matthews Band concert was the next night. Spending just one night away from home took major planning. Packing clothes was easy, but packing medications was complicated and involved careful organization. Early on the morning of the concert, Home I.V. delivered another huge cooler, which we loaded with TPN and medications for our overnight trip and college visit. We were ready to leave by mid-afternoon.

Before we loaded the car, Pastor Hugh came for a visit and a send-off prayer. A few minutes later, Emily announced that she felt a little warm. I took her temperature; the thermometer registered 103.2. I got a second thermometer; it registered 103.6. A third thermometer registered 103.4. Emily and I would not be going to the concert. Instead, we telephoned the on-call doctor and headed for the ER. We all knew that any infection could spell disaster.

It was hard to remain calm during the drive to Charlottesville. As I often did, I inserted Amy Grant's *Songs from the Loft* in the car's tape player. We knew the words to every song and usually sang them as we drove to clinic appointments, but today we just listened. When we crested Afton Mountain, a most amazing thing happened.

We had encountered a hard storm leaving Staunton, but by the time we reached the top of the mountain, the rain had ceased and the sun was shining. As I came down the east side, I noticed a square rainbow outside my window. Emily, who was sitting in the front passenger seat, saw it, too. It traveled with us to the bottom of the

I have set my rainbow in the clouds,

and it will be the sign of the covenant

between me and the earth.

—Genesis 9:13

mountain before disappearing. I'm sure there was a scientific explanation, but never before nor since have I seen a square rainbow. Its presence made chill bumps rise on my arms as I was suddenly wrapped in the promise that God would not forsake us. I became full of peace and free of dread. All was well.

Emily was admitted and started on IV antibiotics. That night we watched news coverage of the concert. Interestingly, Emily never said that she wished she had been there. She felt safe in the hospital. Later that week, she had more surgery to place another bile duct stent.

Since being diagnosed with cancer, Emily had been hospitalized at least a few days every month except in July, August, and September 1994. August 1995 would be another record setter in that, once again, she would have no hospital admissions. She had big plans for the month, too.

Rising seniors usually had their formal yearbook portraits made during the preceding summer. As I prepared to make arrangements for Ann's senior portraits, Emily insisted that she and Sebastian should have their portraits done as well. Appointments were made for all three—Ann, Emily, and Sebastian—for the first week of August. Emily selected her favorite outfit—white tennis shoes, a blue-jeans skirt, and a pink top with imitation pearl buttons and a white silk Peter Pan collar. She topped off her outfit with her black velvet hat and her favorite pewter angel earrings. Sebastian got a bath and grooming. He arrived at the studio wearing a blue bandana around his clean, curly-haired neck.

The photographer was wonderful and very patient. Emily tucked her catheter and morphine tubing behind her so that it would not be visible in the pictures. Sebastian sat on her left side to hide the drainage bag. The biliary stent was working, and the yellowish tint in Emily's skin and eyes had dissipated. To look at the photograph of Emily and Sebastian, one would never suspect that she was desperately ill. Pictures taken with Ann are equally beautiful. They were two sisters whose remaining time together would be far too short. I will be forever grateful that Emily insisted on having these pictures made.

Emily gave wallet-size portraits to most of her friends and many family members, as well as people connected with the hospital.

Naturally, one went to Marta, her beloved hospital teacher. On the back she wrote, "Thank you for being such a good teacher and friend through such hard times. I am glad that I ended up at this hospital so I could meet you and all your great ideas. I hope there are more quilts in my future, but I hope I don't have to do them in here. I appreciate all your hard work. Hope to see you a lot but only on good terms. Thank you for everything! Love, Emily Jones" And on mine, she penned, "To the best, most loving mom a person could have. Love, your one and only Emily Jones."

Emily had a series of clinic visits in August, not only to monitor her status but also to get her ready for her week at Camp Fantastic at the end of the month. Her shots had to be up to date, and she needed a general physical.

During one of the clinic visits, I was asked to step out of the room to speak with the hematology/oncology attending physician. He inquired about our wishes if Emily were to go into cardiac or pulmonary arrest or develop some other medical emergency that could end her life. Jerry and I had already made the heart-wrenching decision that there should be no "heroic" measures to sustain her life. We did not want her intubated or otherwise medicated simply to keep her alive but without quality of life.

When I returned to Emily's clinic room, she immediately questioned me about the discussion that was held outside her hearing. I chose my words carefully, explaining that we requested no intubation or medication in the event of cardiac arrest. I prayed hard that I would never see the request carried out.

In the regular follow-up letter to Dr. Massey that month, that same attending physician referenced the two stents that had been placed to partially relieve the blockage in her biliary system. He also addressed the shift in Emily's pain to "persistent perineal and suprapubic spasms associated with attempts to empty her bladder." He wrote that "we presume that there is some direct invasion of the tumor into the nervous system or compression of peripheral nerves." A cocktail of pain-management drugs was being used to provide relief to Emily. Then he wrote this amazing paragraph:

> Despite all of these challenges, Emily remains in remarkably good spirits and is able to consistently participate in diversional activities, which she finds very satisfying. In addition, Emily's family continues to provide tremendous physical, emotional and spiritual support with only the most subtle signs of fatigue. Much to our surprise, Emily has maintained a stable enough state of health that she is attending Camp Fantastic August 20–26, a special camp for kids with cancer in Front Royal, Va. The camp is staffed with nurses, physicians, and a pharmacist, most of whom practice at NIH in Bethesda, Maryland. In addition, the Home IV care infusional therapy company has bent over backwards to provide Emily what she needs at home as well as for her week at camp. Ten days ago I would never have thought it possible, but now it looks likely that Emily will enjoy a full week away at camp and then start the school year with her peers on 8/28.

In spite of the abundance of medical personnel who would be at Camp Fantastic, Emily was so medically fragile that she was assigned a volunteer nurse who would accompany her to camp. Megan Ibach was a perfect choice. A student nurse at James Madison University, Megan met Emily while doing her pediatric clinical rotation in Charlottesville at the Children's Medical Center. Megan had huge brown eyes and a warm, willing smile. She was intelligent, compassionate, and the best possible companion for Emily during her camp week. It was she who gave Emily the gift of freedom and confidence to be a regular camper. Likewise, Emily gave Megan the gift of personal insight and reflection, intangible but permanent. Years later Megan would write to me:

That sweet, blue-eyed little girl with porcelain skin is on my heart and mind often. Over the years I have reflected quite a bit on life and where I am now relative to where I have been. The experience I had with Emily was not long at all, most definitely not long enough. And yet, the impression she made is enduring.

We live in a society where the loudest people tend to get the most attention. Emily was quite the opposite and it was her quiet demeanor that was the most [impressive]. I had the honor of being assigned as her counselor at Camp Fantastic.

Emily was insightful beyond her years, perplexed and frustrated by her illness but ready to take things as they came. She exhibited patience and endurance, even when obviously feeling poorly, when far bigger an adult would have thrown in the towel. She quietly participated in as many activities at camp that summer as possible and was caught more than once with a huge grin on her face. Offered optional medication as needed for comfort, she chose often to persevere without and fell quietly into bed at night content with the day and exhausted from it. What I remember most about camp were the evenings sitting by her bed with her roommate talking about home, family, faith, and life with cancer. Although hindered by a ravaging illness, Emily certainly did not let it define her. She was her own person, her own spirit; a wonderful testament to fantastic family support even to this day.

I certainly haven't forgotten that precious little girl. I keep a picture of us from that summer in 1995 close. She is ageless and angelic. Although I have certainly grown older since that Polaroid was snapped, the impression she made on me then was clear in my eyes and I look often into my own soul that is so much better for knowing her.

Camp Fantastic was the best thing to happen to Emily that summer. She stared down the direst of circumstances to enjoy a week of feeling completely normal. Jerry and I were told later that Emily's only comment in the camp notebook was one thanking them for a week that allowed her to feel normal. David Smith, camp director, would later write to me that during the week, Emily actually cut back on the number of extra morphine doses that she self-administered during the day. He continues to reference her when he speaks to supporters about the value of Camp Fantastic.

As for me, I had been thrilled that Emily would have the opportunity to go to camp but horrified at the thought of being separated by nearly a hundred miles. Fear that she would die away from her family consumed me in the days before she was to leave. My dear sister paid for a motel room in Front Royal so that I could be within minutes of the camp instead of hours. By the grace of God, the only time I saw Emily all week was at the Thursday-night talent show. In fact, Jerry was with me.

No one told us that parents were not supposed to attend, so Jerry drove to Front Royal for the evening performance. Fortunately, no one asked us to leave. I had my video camera and filmed as much of the show as I could fit on my tape. Emily looked really good and perfectly normal. She stood up straight, moved around freely, and didn't seem to be in pain. She came home energized and ready to start school the following Monday. We had, indeed, received a miracle.

Emily was a goal setter. Just as she was determined to go to Camp Fantastic, she was determined to be a ninth grader at Buffalo Gap High School. She had registered for a full load of classes, some of which would be on the second floor of the school. To make it easier for her, we were loaned a second set of textbooks for home. I met with school administrators to develop a plan should anything happen to Emily on school premises. We also notified the local rescue squad of her status. Jerry met with all her teachers to explain about Emily's fragile condition. One of the teachers was concerned about her doing her homework. Jerry followed up by saying that homework was the least of his worries.

The night before school was to start, Emily became distraught when she had some unexpected vaginal bleeding. I contacted the on-call physician, who directed me on what to do if it got worse. By morning, the bleeding was virtually stopped, and Emily had calmed down. In the warmth of a late August morning, she and Ann got into Ann's Toyota Corolla, and off they went to school.

I had taken the three-month Family Leave option my school system offered, so I did not need to return to teaching for at least that period of time. I never left home that Monday, fearing someone would call with the news that disaster had struck. No one called, and both girls came home happy to have been with friends and ready to tackle the first night's homework assignments.

In spite of increasing episodes of profuse vaginal bleeding, most of which lasted no more than five minutes, Emily managed to continue going to school regularly during September. Of course, she kept her weekly clinic appointments. She also joined friends at several Friday-night football games and was very content. She was, however, extremely jaundiced, and her legs were swelling noticeably.

By the end of September, she was beginning to slow down. At home, I noticed that she took a long time to climb the stairs to her bedroom. More and more frequently, she asked me to take her to school late. I soon realized that her morning classes were on the second floor. When I questioned her, she confessed that she could barely get up the stairs.

Her teachers were wonderful about sending work home or otherwise making it possible for her to keep up. We also moved her from her upstairs bedroom to the family room, where she could sleep on the futon and not have to deal with climbing stairs at home either. Gradually, school became less of a priority. Emily tried hard to keep up but simply wasn't able. A blood transfusion in late September gave her a temporary boost. Shortly thereafter, she had a two-day admission for treatment of cellulitis, a skin infection caused by bacteria.

Pain management became more of an issue. Emily's legs and feet were swelling, and she was given a prescription for compression hose to help reduce fluid buildup. She wore them only a few times; they were hot and tight, and trying to put them on her swollen legs was agonizing for both of us. By this time, Emily went to school only occasionally. She did try to work at home, but it was a struggle for her. Auntie Ann and Lynn came for a visit in early October. Ann wrote to Bubbles later that she and Lynn were so happy that Emily had saved enough energy to sit and talk with them and even go on a grocery store errand.

On October 10, Emily was admitted to the hospital for pain management. The pediatric oncology attending physician noted that she was "a very icteric [jaundiced] young woman in significant pain." Emily quickly made it clear that she had plans to attend Buffalo Gap's Homecoming festivities that weekend. Ann was in the Homecoming Court, and Emily had no intention of missing the game. The attending doctor wrote in his chart note, "knowing her determination we will plan on it."

We were honored and thrilled that Ann had been nominated for the Buffalo Gap High School Homecoming Court that year. I don't think Emily cared much about seeing the game Friday night, but she was desperate to be there for the halftime parade and the crowning of the Homecoming King and Queen.

Dr. Dunsmore promised Emily that she would be home in time to see it. She kept her promise: Emily was discharged Friday afternoon. She was given a prescription for a wheelchair, which was delivered that same day.

Friday night found her sitting in her wheelchair on the sidelines of the Buffalo Gap football field. The air was crisp, and wispy, white breath escaped from her mouth when she talked. She watched the Homecoming parade and clapped when "Princess Ann" and Andy, her escort, were announced. Tears streamed down Emily's face. A young girl whom I had tutored happened to see her crying and asked her what was wrong. "These are tears of joy," Emily whispered.

Auntie Carol, Jerry's sister, was visiting that night and went to the football game with us. I took a picture of her and Emily in the car after the game. It is the saddest picture that I ever made of my precious daughter. She was so thin and extremely yellow. Her cheeks were getting puffy from extended steroid use. Her hair had grown back in curly and a deep auburn. She had a knitted tam on her head and a tennis sweater over her turtleneck shirt. You can't see it in the picture, but she had on blue jeans and kept a blanket over her legs to help her stay warm.

The following day, I enjoyed helping Ann get ready for the Homecoming dance. Emily now spent most of her time sitting Indian-style on the futon, watching television and talking with whoever happened to be nearby. She never lacked for company. Sebastian loved curling up beside her for tummy rubs. Emily used Tuppie as a pillow to support her head, even though that sweet seal's soft white fur had gotten stained over the months. Tuppie was never more than an arm's length from Emily and never missed a hospitalization.

Susan Shipp, our Home I.V. nurse, was at our house working with Emily when Ann descended the stairs, dressed in her formal gown, with her hair styled and her makeup carefully applied. Andy was waiting in the living room. Bubbles sat on the futon with Emily and Sebastian. Emily's back was to me. Susan later told me that the look on Emily's face revealed both complete acceptance and heart-wrenching sadness that she would never go to a Homecoming dance. Even as I write this, my heart aches for all the things that Emily never got to do.

Emily never blamed Ann, and, so far as I know, she never took out her disappointments on her sister. Emily only had words of support and love for her sister, whose life was totally normal, just as it should be. I believe that Emily's life was as normal as possible, in part because Ann's life was normal.

1995

Because Emily's port was beneath her skin and had to be accessed by a nurse, Jerry and I discussed the possibility of replacing it with an outside (double lumen) port so we could manage medications better at home. The oncology team agreed, and a two-day admission was planned for the end of the month. One afternoon, a week or so prior to the admission, Emily and I were in the family room watching television. She sat on the futon, and I was behind her in a recliner, which had become my bed since Emily no longer went upstairs.

Without provocation, Emily turned to me and said, "Mom, I'm ready to write my will." Months earlier, I had cautiously asked her to tell me what her wishes would be in the event she did not get her miracle. She was not interested, and I never brought up the subject again. I grabbed a pen and some scratch paper and began writing the names dictated to me. After she completed the list, which included friends and family, she began to tell me who would get her most treasured items.

Auntie Ann, she said, was to have her hat collection. David Kleiner, who had helped her write "Cancer for Christmas," was to get a small guitar charm. Her Cabbage Patch dolls were to go to her dearest family and friends. Tuppie was to be mine. Emily said of her clothes, "Give them to someone who needs them." And so it went through the first twenty or so names on the list. Then she said, "You do the rest, Mom." I promised that I would, then placed the list by the phone next to my recliner.

As planned, Emily was admitted for the replacement of her port with a central line. The following day, we received instruction in its care and were sent home. Halloween was the next Tuesday. Katie and her mom came over after school so that Katie could help Emily hand out candy. They played Christmas music and giggled while answering the door. Katie was so good for Emily. She knew exactly how to cheer her up and help her relax and feel normal. There it is again—feeling normal; that's really all that Emily desired.

By around eight thirty, all the ghosts, goblins, princesses, and pirates had left the neighborhood. Katie and her mom left, too, and Emily returned to the futon and Tuppie to watch television and eat a little leftover candy. I know she was exhausted and uncomfortable, but she'd had a good time, and that was really all that mattered.

Over the next two days, the weakness in Emily's legs became much more apparent. They were swollen, and there were prominent stretch marks on her upper thighs. Just as she had walked laps on the seventh floor, I had encouraged her to exercise in our house by walking laps through the living room, dining room, and kitchen. Often she would make five or six loops several times during the day, but now she was no longer able to manage that routine.

She had a clinic appointment on November 2. Her weakness was obvious, and she was admitted to the hospital the next day. Her admission examination noted multiple bruises and petechiae (pinpoint spots from bleeding under the skin) over her back. We had noticed them as well. I think they were a side effect of long-term steroid use. No bowel sounds were heard in her gut, either.

Several months earlier, we had tried to wean Emily off steroids, but it was a disaster. We knew there would be increasing negative side-effects, but we agreed to deal with them rather than subject her to pain that was more than she could tolerate.

Emily was given multiple blood products, including three units of packed red blood cells and two units of platelets during her seven-day admission. All sorts of medications were started to deal with infection, gastrointestinal bleeding, and abdominal pain. Her morphine dosage was increased. She was given one more unit of platelets before she was discharged on November 9.

During the latter part of the week that Emily was an inpatient, the HEP had another special event, this one with the visiting US

Olympic women's basketball team, which was traveling throughout the United States playing college teams in preparation for the 1996 Summer Olympics. That weekend, they were to play the UVA women's team.

Emily sat on a bench on the terrace. She talked to most of the athletes, but one beautiful player in particular took a special interest in her. Jennifer Azzi knelt down on the floor beside her and soon they were deep in conversation. Before the event was over, she had invited Emily to attend the game at U-Hall, as the Cavaliers' basketball arena was fondly called.

The next day, a package containing one of Jennifer's warm-up suits and a sweet note arrived for Emily. She was too exhausted to go to the game on Friday, but the next week we did watch a televised game of the Olympic women playing against Stanford. Afterward, I wrote Jennifer a long letter explaining about Emily's cancer and thanking her for taking Emily into her life and heart. The following summer, Jennifer and her teammates did win gold medals in Atlanta.

Thanksgiving 1995 found our house full of family and friends and good food. The Christmas tree was up and decorated, which added to the festive mood. Emily, who was horribly yellow and puffy, was unable to eat, but she remained in the thick of things at her futon "campsite." Sebastian and Tuppie were always by her side. Conversation was upbeat and happy. Laughter filled the rooms as we ate our fill and talked to Emily.

Jerry's family returned home on Thursday night, but Auntie Ann and Lynn stayed until Saturday morning. They had lots of questions for Emily, who answered them with poise and grace. On "black" Friday, they stayed with Emily so that Bubbles and I could do a bit of shopping. Jerry and I also got away alone to make a couple of purchases. I was never comfortable being away from Emily for long and was happy to return home late Friday afternoon. Cell phones didn't exist in those days, so getting in touch with me in an emergency was almost impossible.

Auntie Ann was particularly touched by the relationship between Emily and Sebastian. Some weeks later, she wrote in a letter to Bubbles, "Just watching Emily scratch his ear or pat him on the head spoke volumes about her love for him. That was evident even at Thanksgiving when she was so weak."

Before the month was out, Karen, my colleague and constant prayer warrior, would send this handwritten note to Emily: "Then as suddenly as his trial began, Job's test was over. So will it be for you, Emily. AND Job's end was greater than his beginning. So will it be for you, Emily. Job was richer than he had ever been—not just in family and possessions, but in his knowledge of his Redeemer."

1995

Chapter 14

There's wind blowing on me.

—Emily, from her hospital bed,
December 14, 1995

November slipped imperceptibly into December. The first days were cold and clear. Staunton's annual Christmas parade was to be held the first Monday of the month. Friends who owned a small downtown bed-and-breakfast hotel on the parade route invited Emily to come there to watch the parade so that she could stay out of the cold.

We hadn't realized until we got there that she would have to climb one flight of steps to get to the viewing area. Emily struggled to get to the top. She tried to smile and seem as though she were enjoying the parade, but looking back, I know she was in agony. She tried so very hard to be and do just what she always had been and done—by that time more for us than for herself.

On the morning after the parade, Emily had been invited to participate in a special presentation of the Adolescent Quilting Project at Grand Rounds, which would be held at the Kluge Children's Rehabilitation Center (KCRC). While KCRC was part of the Children's Medical Center, it was located in a separate building just west of Charlottesville. The facility had an adjacent parking lot, which meant that it would be much easier to get her into this building than into the main hospital.

Jerry and I were particularly pleased to be going, because the KCRC held special memories for us. It was there that Jerry and I had met in mid-October 1970, when it was called simply the Children's Rehabilitation Center (CRC). As undergraduates at the University of Virginia, we had separately signed up to volunteer at the CRC. Whether through a random occurrence or divine intervention, we were scheduled for volunteer orientation on the same day. We remember it vividly. I even remember that I wore a pale-green skirt and matching sweater, Pappagallo flats, and had my long, deep-brown hair pulled back and tied with green yarn at the crown of my head. I was also wearing the coolest, very "hip," octagonal glasses.

While it wasn't love at first sight, it was definitely like at first sight. Jerry and I were amazingly compatible, and we enjoyed volunteering on the same days as much as our schedules allowed. Many of our early dates included CRC patients who were allowed to leave the center for special events. By Christmas, Jerry and I had become just about inseparable.

I remember Jerry's first Christmas present to me. I had been hoping for a ring, but the beautifully wrapped box was too big for that. I opened it to find a plain, white china egg. When I lifted the lid, though, I saw that it was filled with beautiful china violets. Jerry said I was like that egg—a little plain on the outside but filled with flowers on the inside. I knew I was rather plain, but no one had ever before told me that I was colorful and vibrant on the inside.

We were married two Christmases later—December 16, 1972—at University Chapel. It might have been one of the coldest, windiest nights on record, but it made little difference to me. I was too head-over-heels in love with this wonderful man to care about the weather. Now, close to twenty-three years later, we were coming back to where it had begun for us. We were excited to share our story with Emily.

Emily put enormous effort into getting ready the morning of Grand Rounds. Just standing to brush her teeth took great energy. She selected a cheerful, loose-fitting Christmas sweatshirt to wear with her soft sweat pants. She kept a quilt over her lap and legs for extra warmth. Her hair, which had grown in curly and a beautiful, rich auburn color, framed her face. Her cheeks were steroid-puffy to the point that she didn't especially look like herself and smiling was not comfortable. She was yellow, especially the whites of her eyes. She had to rest after getting dressed. Transferring from the futon to her wheelchair was clearly painful. Even getting enough breath support to speak above a whisper was hard for her. Still, she was determined to go to Grand Rounds.

We pulled into the KCRC patient parking area and opened the door for Emily. I can still see the pain that stretched across her face as she forced herself to stand and pivot from car to wheelchair that cold, gray morning. She wouldn't allow anyone to touch her. All we could do was watch—helpless parental sentinels—as she eased herself into her chair and used her arms to prop herself up for better breathing.

We rode the elevator up one level to the main floor and entered the gym, which was packed with medical staff and invited guests. It was noisy but festive. Musicians were warming up as Marta Gilliam, who would emcee the event, made last-minute program adjustments. Theresa Andrews met us in the gym and sat beside Emily throughout the program, which lasted more than an hour. Someone tied red and green Christmas balloons to the back of Emily's wheelchair. Emily had been invited to speak, but she declined. Watching was sufficient for her.

The program was video recorded, and a personalized copy was given to us. In addition to the full Grand Rounds presentation, it includes personal interviews with Emily and with Marta. When I look at the videotape now, I am consumed with sadness and grief for my daughter, who was in such pain that little sighs occasionally slipped from her lips as she tried to answer questions.

Early in the interview, she was asked why attending the quilt show was so important. She responded that the CMC people meant a great deal to her and that she appreciated how they had cheered her up when she was in the hospital. It was important, she said, to show our appreciation to them. She also talked about the meaning of her Pandora quilt. "All Pandora had left in her box was hope," she said. "Then I realized that all some cancer kids have a lot of times is their hope. You can always keep your hope up."

"Tell me a little bit about the hope are you holding on to," the interviewer said.

"That I am healed," answered Emily. A few minutes later she said, "You always have hope. Just never give up."

Emily went on to talk about her song, "Cancer for Christmas." She repeated that it was important for people to understand that anyone could get "this disease" and that, even though it wasn't fair, life *had* to go on. Her interview concluded with a discussion of her friendship with Dave Matthews. She confirmed that he called her occasionally and that he really did have her phone number written on his shoe. After just a few more questions, Emily's final interview had come to an end. It was time to go home. Emily, however, begged for a tour of the building. Jerry and I thought she was interested in our story, but she was really just trying to delay having to get herself back into the car.

December 7 was a turning point in our lives. It had snowed the night before, and there was no school in Augusta County, which meant all five of us were at home. As she did most mornings, Emily started to walk her laps around the main floor of the house. She made it from the family room to the living room—a distance of not more than twenty feet—then grabbed a chair. She turned and said that she could go no farther. I helped her back to the recliner in the family room.

That's when I saw the jagged patch of red on the inside of her right thigh. I immediately called Susan Shipp. She arrived within minutes and, looking at the ugly redness, told us what we already knew: the patch was cellulitis. To monitor it, she used a ball-point pen to outline the perimeter before she left. She planned to return in the evening to make another assessment.

Our doorbell rang while Susan worked with Emily. I opened it to Emily's good friend, Dave Matthews. Earlier in the morning, he had called to see if Emily felt like having a visitor. He wasn't intimidated by the snow. In fact, he said, he had just purchased a new Subaru Outback and wanted to try it out. So there he was in our house. He sat and talked to Bubbles and us until Susan finished, then that dear man took out his acoustic guitar, sat beside Emily, and played and sang for her.

Years later, in the movie *Because of Winn-Dixie*, he would play the part of Otis, a guitar-playing ex-con who has a special way with some crazy pet store animals. At one point, the animals get out of their cages and pens and run amok. Otis takes out his guitar and sings a gentle, sweet song. As Otis caresses his guitar strings, the animals settle, and the craziness comes to a halt. Opal (AnnaSophia Robb), the lonely ten-year-old sweetheart who has befriended Otis, slips in unnoticed and listens. It is a very moving, tender part of the movie. I cannot see it without thinking of the day Dave played and sang to Emily. His gentle, sweet song was a soothing balm to her. She smiled when he was done.

Dave stayed for several hours, then was gone. I fixed lunch, and we hung out in the family room near the recliner, where Emily sat covered with her angel blanket. She had not moved since getting into the chair that morning. I had not checked the status of her cellulitis.

After lunch, she insisted that we watch a family movie. *Forrest*

Gump was her choice. Emily had seen it many times, but she held fast that we should watch it together on this afternoon.

Looking back, I am convinced that Emily sent little messages to us through her choice of movies. For example, right after she was diagnosed with cancer, she insisted on watching *Steel Magnolias*. In fact, that movie was the first one that we purchased for her. In the film, Shelby (Julia Roberts), the brittle diabetic daughter, dies. Her death is traumatic and sad, and her mother, M'Lynn (Sally Field), falls apart at her daughter's tragic and untimely passing. We will never know for certain whether Emily was sending a subtle, blatant, or meaningless message to us by expressing interest in that film.

A particular scene in *Forrest Gump* may also have conveyed a message that Emily could not express for herself. It happens when Forrest's mother is nearing death. Forrest, who is sitting beside her bed, sees that she is unafraid. She smiles and says, "Forrest, everybody has a time to die, and this is my time." The next scene opens with Forrest putting flowers on her grave in the cemetery.

Sometime before Thanksgiving, Emily had asked that we put a lighted swag Christmas decoration across the fence at the front of the house. She drew a simple picture of what she wanted, showed it to Jerry, and watched from the living room window as the swag was meticulously hung according to her plan. She had not been outside to see it lit up at night, however.

On the afternoon of December 7, when darkness wasn't far away, we turned on the Christmas tree and swag lights. The swag was especially pretty against the backdrop of new snow. Shortly after dark, there came another knock on our door. It was Abi Henneberry, Emily's beloved first dance teacher. Abi and her husband had moved to Canada. She and her two daughters were back visiting her mother, who would eventually join Abi in Canada but at this time still lived in the Valley.

We were deeply moved that Abi had set aside time to visit Emily, who perked up at hearing her voice. Always cheerful, Abi introduced her two children to Emily, then chatted about life in Alberta. She stayed only a few minutes, perhaps because she realized how sick Emily was or because "incorrigible Sebastian" did what he sometimes did when company came—he passed gas. I remember commenting that neither of her children had coats. Her younger child was still in an infant carrier and wasn't even covered by a blanket. Not to worry, said Abi. Living where cold is really cold made Virginia's temperature seem more like a Canadian spring.

Within minutes of Abi's departure, Susan returned to check on Emily's cellulitis. I was shocked when I saw that the infection had burst past the ball-point perimeter and had spread about halfway down the back of her leg. I knew we had a serious situation on our hands. Susan called the hospital to inform them that we were coming, as I began to make preparations for our trip to the ER.

Emily was in terrible, terrible pain. I hit the "override" button on her morphine pump every six minutes to administer the maximum dose allowed by her doctors. Things were happening so fast, yet so painfully slowly. Well before this medical crisis occurred, Jerry had asked Emily if she would prefer to remain at home or go to the hospital when "the time came." Her choice was to go to the hospital. Emily was the only one not crying.

I brought the wheelchair beside the futon and locked the brakes. She wouldn't let anyone touch her. It took at least fifteen agonizing minutes for her to make the transfer from futon to wheelchair. Jerry remembers with great sadness her sighs of pain. After she was settled in her chair, Ann knelt in front of her to try to get shoes on her swollen feet. Sebastian sat beside Emily's chair looking up at her. As Ann worked, she felt Emily's hand on her shoulder. "I'm going to be okay," Emily whispered. Ann wept even harder.

The night air was very cold, so before we left the house, I wrapped my red flannel cape around Emily's frail, thin shoulders. We eased her out the back door and down the ramp to the driveway, where Jerry had the heated van waiting. It took her another fifteen to twenty minutes to transfer from her wheelchair into the front seat.

After what seemed like an interminably long time, Jerry finally backed out of the driveway and down the street so that Emily could see the lighted swag that she had designed. "Daddy, it's beautiful," she said as she leaned her head against the headrest and closed her eyes. Every few minutes, she reminded me to push the button for more morphine, and that is exactly what I did—over and over and over again.

Someone with a gurney was waiting for us at the ER. Again, Emily stopped anyone from touching her. It took another thirty excruciating minutes before she could get out of the car and onto the stretcher. I have no memory of what we did in the ER. Jerry remembers trying to get her to talk to the nurse about Dave Matthews's visit earlier that day to get her mind off her pain. Finally, by sometime in the wee hours of Friday morning, December 8, Emily was resting in hospital room 7151.

I quickly hung her paper angels from the ceiling IV pole as I had done at every admission since she had received them. For the next twenty-four hours, she remained almost motionless, wrapped in my red cape and wearing her street clothes, searing pain enveloping her even with mega doses of morphine.

By Saturday morning, Emily had stabilized and was doing better. Even though she had developed a cough, the tortured look was gone from her face. Earlier, she had allowed me to remove my cape and her clothes and replace them with a soft, comfortable hospital gown. It was then that I noticed a profusion of tiny purple spots across her back. Her legs were still very swollen and more stretch marks had formed on her thighs.

Not until I read her medical record in preparation for writing this book did I learn the full extent of her diagnosis at admission. Her primary diagnosis was cellulitis, which may have traveled from her bowel. Her secondary diagnosis included pleural effusion, thrush, a decubitus ulcer (bedsore) on her left buttock, post hemorrhagic anemia, renal failure, malignant neoplasm, gastrointestinal hemorrhage, malignant small bowel adenocarcinoma, and E-coli infection. I now believe that her strong spirit and unshakable conviction in complete healing was all that had kept her alive.

Sometime later Saturday, I left a dozing Emily to go into the seventh floor conference room to make a few phone calls. Dr. De Alarcon, who was on call, came into the room, tears streaming down his cheeks. "You know how I promised that I would tell you when Emily would not go home again," he said, as hot tears began to burn my own eyes in anticipation of what was coming. "I am telling you that Emily will not go home again," he wept.

"I wanted my miracle," I sobbed. "I wanted my miracle."

"You got your miracle," he said with gentleness and compassion. "Most adults with this cancer live four to five months. Emily has lived nearly two years."

He said:

"In my distress I called to the Lord,

and he answered me.

From the depths of the grave I called for help,

And you listened to my cry."

—Jonah 2:2

Dr. De Alarcon remained with me while I composed myself. Looking back, I am in awe of Emily's team of doctors, all of whom were sensitive and loving. Dr. De Alarcon would write to me years later, "There are people who during their life make such an impression that they are never far in our minds and hearts. Emily is one of those people. There are little stories—from the day she and my daughter Tessa rowed [a] canoe, to her messages to our team during [her] last weeks—that remain with me. She was so smart and self-possessed!"

೮

Because Emily was in such terrible shape, a bedside potty chair was ordered for her hospital room so that she would not have to walk even the few steps into her bathroom. We'd had a potty chair at home for months, but blockages had totally stopped her bowel function. You can imagine my surprise when, Saturday evening, she sat up in bed and said she had to go. As hard as it was for her to move, she sat on the potty chair. Minutes later she announced that she "had gone." There was great significance to this event. I believe that God was fulfilling a specific prophecy given to Emily weeks earlier.

Although I am not positive of the timeframe, I think it was during early summer of that year that a deeply faith-filled teacher colleague from the middle school began making regular visits to Emily. Gary Persinger and Emily had many serious conversations about her faith, healing, and the power of prayer, especially prayer spoken in tongues. He frequently prayed for Emily in tongues and encouraged her to do the same.

One Sunday afternoon, Gary showed up at the house after an absence of several weeks. He had a big grin on his face when I answered the door. He said that he hadn't wanted to come until he knew for sure that his word of knowledge was from the Lord. He was ready to share it with Emily. She was sitting on the futon. Beside her was the potty chair that we had gotten for home use. Gary asked if he could pray for her in tongues, to which she agreed.

I was sitting in the recliner near the futon and listened as Gary prayed in a language foreign to us but known to God. It actually sounded like Japanese. Interpretation in English followed every few lines spoken in tongues. God spoke directly to Emily through Gary, giving her three distinct messages. He said that He had placed an almond branch over her head and that He was faithful to perform His word. He said that He was well pleased with her and that many would come to Him through her. Finally, he said that her cancer would pass out of her body through her bowel.

I looked at Gary and asked, "How will we know when her cancer passes out of her bowel?"

"You will know," he promised.

There before me in a hospital potty chair was certainly the fulfillment of that prophecy. Over the next twenty-four hours, it happened four more times. With as much boldness as I could muster, I shared the prophecy with the attending physician, who said he would send the "next one" to the lab for testing. The next one came, but its appearance was different. As ordered, it was sent to the lab, where it was determined to be a blood clot. I'm sure it *was* just a blood clot, but I'm just as sure that the first five were cancer passing out of Emily's body through her bowel. God was indeed faithful to perform His word.

Emily became weaker over the next several days. She was given oxygen support and blood to replace what she was losing through hemorrhaging. Several unsuccessful attempts were made to place a Duoderm patch over the bedsore. Emily was on so much morphine that she probably wasn't even aware of pain. She never complained about it.

Wednesday morning brought with it a surprise from Nancy Artis. A beautiful little boxwood Christmas tree was delivered to Emily's hospital room. It was covered in red bows. Shortly after it arrived, Nancy stopped by to say that Emily simply had to have her own Christmas tree. Emily loved it. From her hospital bed she directed me in rearranging many of the little red bows until it was exactly as she wanted it.

A bright blue angel flag hung from the wall-mounted television set at the foot of her bed. Emily had insisted that Bubbles purchase it as an early Christmas present for me. I was moved to tears when I unwrapped her package and saw the beautiful angel, whose eyes are closed and hands opened at her side, as though she were offering a blessing. She floats on a dark-blue background with gold stars around her. Emily's unspoken message was clear: "Don't worry, Mom. Soon everything will be okay." To this day, when I look upon "Emily's angel," I know that everything *is* okay.

Early Wednesday afternoon, Auntie Ann and Lynn came for a visit. They had traveled from their home in Pennsylvania, arriving in Charlottesville just ahead of bad weather. Lynn brought Emily a beautiful angel with a sweeping skirt and china hands and head, which was encircled by a tiny wreath. She could be plugged in so that soft lights illuminated her from within, to me a reminder of how the Holy Spirit illuminated Emily. Lynn's angel remained lit day and night for the remainder of Emily's life. She has been included in our holiday decorations every Christmas since.

Emily, Auntie Ann, Lynn, Jerry, and I had a supremely wonderful visit that afternoon in our little hospital Christmas haven. It was the last time Emily would see Auntie Ann and Lynn. By nightfall, an ice storm was in full throttle, and the hospital seemed almost deserted except for patient families padding through the carpeted halls. The quiet was almost eerie. Emily and I were watching television when in strolled Pastor Hugh from our church in Staunton.

"Hugh, what are you doing here?" I exclaimed.

"I came to anoint Emily and pray for her," he replied, a smile on his face.

I simply could not believe that anyone had ventured out on such a dreadful night. Hugh said that cars had been in the ditch on both sides of the road, but he never even slipped.

"Oh, dear," I thought to myself. "He's had a word of knowledge that Emily is going to die tonight." Such a thought had not crossed my mind until that moment. I desperately fought against it now, as

I could not bear to think that Emily would die with only me, and perhaps Hugh, by her side. Emily may have had the same thought, because she flatly refused his prayer.

He said again that he wanted to anoint and pray for Emily. She continued to shake her head "no." Of course, the only choice I had was to insist that Emily welcome Hugh's prayer, especially since he had risked life and limb to get to Charlottesville for this specific purpose. Emily relented and gave her consent.

I stood at the head of the bed on her right side, underneath her paper angels. Hugh placed blessed oil on his fingers and touched Emily. As I stood holding Emily's hands in prayer, I was immediately aware of being surrounded by the Holy Spirit. It was tangible and wonderful, and I didn't want the Presence to leave me. When Hugh ended his prayer, the Presence was gone. I said nothing about my experience to him or to Emily.

The next day, Hugh called me on the phone. He said that when he looked up from praying for Emily, he saw the aura of angels, one standing on each side of Emily's bed. Tears welled up in my eyes. I hadn't seen them with my earthly eyes, but my spirit recognized them fully. They were real. I do not know their purpose, but they were there.

From that day forward, Emily would say at random times, "There's wind blowing on me. There's wind blowing on me." We faithfully checked to make sure wind was not blowing directly on her. We finally decided that holy wind from the wings of angels was blowing on Emily. Jerry felt their presence so strongly in her room that he often looked over her bed to see if he could catch a glimpse of them. He could not. But they were there.

Many years later, I learned that "Angels among Us" was one of Emily's favorite songs and that she sang it often in her high school choral group. Kathy Rowe, the Buffalo Gap High School choral director, wrote regarding Emily's love for this song,

During Emily's last weeks of her journey on earth, she struggled to enter the classroom, would find her seat, and without any help from her friends (Emily was very independent) would get her music folder out. The class always wanted to sing one of Emily's favorite songs, "Angels among Us"! As the beautiful voices sang the beautiful lyrics to this song—*I believe there are angels among us*—it was [as] if Emily knew these were her final hours and angels were surrounding her and comforting her as she traveled from this world to the next! Without a tear, she would continue singing until her strength gave out. . . . even though Emily did not notice the many friends' tears around her. . . . and I must say that I choked on my own tears trying to give strength to Emily and the rest of the class! Little did Emily know she was showing me strength instead!

Angels among us, indeed!

Jerry and I celebrated our twenty-third wedding anniversary on Saturday, December 16. During the afternoon, we received an absolutely wonderful anniversary gift. David Kleiner popped into Emily's room, and in his hand he held a copy of her finished song, "Cancer for Christmas" (pages 246–47). He said that the musicians had gotten together in a local studio to record the song. In doing so, they'd sort of sidestepped protocol. They knew as well as the rest of us that without a miracle, Emily did not have time to wait for the full legal process of producing a CD to unfold. We sat mesmerized as he played the recording for us. It was incredible.

The version of "Cancer for Christmas" that was recorded that morning is the exact version that was later included on the CD entitled *Pandora's Box—Songs of Hope*. A picture of Emily's Pandora quilt is on the cover of the album. This ingenious album was a collection of songs written by adolescent patients at the Children's Medical Center, University of Virginia Hospital, in collaboration with musicians and writers from the Charlottesville community. It was recorded locally and produced by the Hospital Education Program.

Emily loved her song. It said exactly what she wanted people to hear about cancer and specifically about *her* cancer. In my wildest dreams, I would not have imagined that at the age of fourteen my daughter would become an author and now a published songwriter. When Emily had first learned that she had a rarest-of-rare form of childhood cancer, she'd said she would be famous. She could not possibly have known just how many lives she had touched and would continue to touch, exactly as she was told by God.

Wanting to give us dinner-date time for our anniversary, Bubbles, Elmer, and Ocie came to stay with Emily while Jerry and I went out to eat. We selected a favorite seafood restaurant not too far from the hospital. Emily was pleased to have her grandparents stay with her. This would be the last time she would ever see her beloved Bubbles, PawPaw, and MeeMaw.

Sunday dawned clear and cold. During the long afternoon, many people came to see Emily. One was my dear college friend, Karen McCarron. It was her son, Ryan, who had attended Emily's first *en pointe* appearance in *The Nutcracker* two years earlier. Karen visited with Emily and me in the room, then asked me to join her outside for a few minutes. We went to one of the general waiting rooms on the seventh floor, where Karen wept bitterly. I supported her as best I could. I was used to seeing Emily's wasted little body and forgot how hard it was for friends and family who had not seen her in several months. I did remind myself often that Emily's spiritual healing was perfect and that I must not be deceived by what my physical eyes were witnessing.

About a month after Emily died, Karen called to tell me that she had been awakened sometime during a previous night. Sitting up in bed, she saw an illuminated purple cross float in through the door to the bedroom. It floated across the room and lay down on an antique humpback trunk at the foot of her bed. Karen thought to herself, "That is Emily." She returned to sleep with the cross still resting on the trunk. It was gone in the morning, but the memory remains with Karen to this day.

Throughout that Sunday, Emily was losing blood at an alarming rate; she was given packed cells during the evening after all her visitors were gone. Emily made Monday "Mom's Shopping Day." She had made a mental list of people for whom she wanted to get Christmas gifts and sent me out to local stores to make the purchases. I dashed between mall department stores, looking for items that matched her descriptions as closely as possible, then dashed back to the hospital to show her.

"That's perfect. . . . No, that's got to go back. . . . That will do." This went on throughout the day. I was tired by suppertime but would have gladly shopped all night if need be. By evening, however, she was content with her purchases. The next day, I wrapped them, and she tried to write the tags. She struggled to control the pen, however, and eventually asked me to do it for her.

Jerry stayed with Emily while I shopped. He remembers two very distinct things about that day: sensing angels over Emily's bed and being overwhelmed by an extremely unpleasant smell. He told me days later that it was the smell of death. It was so pervasive that he asked the nurses to remove all the trash bins from Emily's room. Through all of this, Emily kept saying that wind was blowing on her. I am absolutely sure it was.

On Tuesday, we learned that Emily would be started on insulin; she would have her blood sugar checked several times a day. I sat by her bed and sobbed when a nurse came to stick her finger. Emily looked at me with incredibly sad and accepting eyes and said, "Don't worry, Mom. I can't even feel it." I cried harder. This child had been poked and prodded until it seemed to me that little else was possible.

She was hemorrhaging from everywhere. The stretch marks on her leg had burst open and were draining so profusely that she

Lessons from Emily

would soak the bed in about twenty minutes. Every time we tried to move her, purple imprints of our hands were left on her skin. The burn team was called to help move her so wet sheets could be changed, but their efforts, gentle as they were, left more purple marks. I finally suggested using diapers to soak up the fluid. This solution worked, and we no longer had to move Emily.

In all, eight different machines were running by Emily's bedside—oxygen, morphine, antibiotics, blood products, and who knows what else. Sometime during the day, the doctors asked if we wanted them to turn off the machines. Jerry's reply was adamant, "No. Emily has not given up, so neither have we." We kept vigil by her bed into the evening. Sometime after dark, the phone rang. Emily, who was weak beyond description, answered it. I could tell immediately that Gary Persinger was on the other end, praying with Emily and encouraging her. Then I heard her repeat over and over into the receiver, "By His stripes I am healed. By His stripes I am healed."

Well into the evening, Jerry decided to return to the hotel to try to get some rest. He had to tease and coax Emily to get her to even say good-night to him. This was totally unlike Emily. After he left, she returned to saying, "By his stripes I am healed." Those were the only words I heard from her for the remainder of the night.

Chapter 15

I'll make it.

—*quote from a tiny stick figure*
nearing the top of a steep hill
in a drawing by Emily during her illness

Around two in the morning on Wednesday, December 20, a resident physician stepped into Emily's room and asked to speak to me in the hall. Once outside, he told me that her death was imminent, and he wanted to know if the family was prepared. I looked at him and said the only thing I knew to say, "She doesn't expect to die, and I will support her." He nodded and left; I returned to Emily's room. She was resting and did not ask me about the conversation. I went back to the parent bed and tried to sleep.

Several hours later, a nurse called Jerry at the hotel and suggested that he come as quickly as possible. At the same time, they told me that the time had come to call in family. Another ice storm had hit the area overnight, and I was not sure that anyone could even get to the hospital.

Augusta County Schools were in session, however, so I called Buffalo Gap High School and asked to speak to Koressa Malcolm, the school's psychologist and the dear friend who provided Sebastian's doggie camp. I explained to Koressa what was happening and asked her to find Ann and Andy and ask if they wanted to come to the hospital. She would bring them if they did. Andy's parents gave permission, and they were soon on their way to Charlottesville. I prayed they would be in time.

I also called my mom. She would stay at home to take phone calls.

Jerry checked out of the hotel, knowing he would not be back. He arrived at the hospital around nine o'clock. We went to Emily's room together and sat beside her. She opened her eyes and looked directly at us and said, "I am going to die. I'm sorry." We knew the time had come to ask the nurse to turn off as many machines as possible. With that, the room became strangely quiet except for the soft whir of oxygen and a single IV pump.

For nearly two years, this strong, wonderful angel had protected her parents from any additional pain or agony. Now, on a crystal clear morning, the last day of fall, we were free to share openly with our precious daughter our beliefs about heaven. We told her that Jesus himself was waiting for her and that our one regret was that we could not go with her. We told her how proud we were of her, that it was okay to go, that she was not letting us down.

It was clear that breathing had become harder for her, and she was restless. Then, after she rested for a few minutes, I heard her say, "My papers. My papers."

I grabbed the latest set of scriptures sent to me by Karen and Sharon. "Do you mean these, Emily?" I said, desperation edging into my voice.

"My papers. My papers," she repeated.

As my mind raced, I looked everywhere for papers. I pulled more scripture references from my Bible to show her, but I still had not found what it was that she was referencing. The Lord then quickened to my mind that she was talking about her will. I had written it on scraps of paper and left them by the phone in the family room. They had remained there since October.

"You mean your will, Emily! Yes, I will take care of it for you. Your papers are safe." She remained calm for a few minutes, and then said, "My baby. My baby." Again, I searched the room trying to figure out what she was referencing. And again she said, "My baby. My baby." Then I realized that Tuppie had gotten pushed to the bottom of the bed.

"You mean Tuppie, Emily? Here she is. Tuppie is right here."

I handed the beloved, soft, stained seal to her. She cradled Tuppie in her arms and slowly rocked her back and forth. This loving, kind, gentle act—as tender and sweet as a mother cuddling her newborn baby—was Emily's last. She had no more strength to speak. With the energy left to her, she picked at the covers and oxygen cup that rested on her chest. We asked Dr. Dunsmore to give her something that would help calm her. A nurse administered a medication, and soon Emily was still and breathing slowly and comfortably. We tucked Tuppie under her long, slender hands. Dr. Dunsmore later assured me that Emily could hear us but was unable to respond due to the medication.

Ann, Andy, and Koressa arrived by late morning. They were delayed due to an electric line that had fallen across the interstate during the previous night's storm. Koressa was preparing to flag down a state trooper for assistance when traffic was allowed to move.

Once at Emily's bedside, Ann took Emily's hand and caressed it gently and spoke sweet, loving words to her sister. Ann and Andy's tears fell and fell and fell. Dr. Dunsmore entered Emily's room. She, too, was weeping. She told Emily how much she loved her. More and more people came into the room and said the same. Pastor Hugh came. Shortly after, Steve Huffer, another of the faithful prayer warriors from our church, arrived. I couldn't imagine how Steve knew to come. He shrugged and said, "I just knew."

In the early afternoon, Hugh led us in singing Emily's favorite praise songs. He then read aloud Psalm 23, rephrasing it so that it was specific to Emily. Around one thirty, there was a distinct change in Emily's breathing. Everyone in the room became very quiet as we waited with her. A few minutes later, Jerry stood up and walked to her side. He leaned down, said he loved her, kissed her good-bye, and whispered what I have come to call the Gospel according to Jiminy Cricket: "See you later." In those three words, Jerry spoke his confidence that Jesus the Christ died for us, that we have the hope of heaven through Him, and that we will see Emily again.

> Jesus said, "Let the little children come to me, and do not hinder them, for the kingdom of heaven belongs to such as these."
>
> —Matthew 19:14

Teardrops slipped from Emily's eyes almost immediately after Jerry spoke. Then, as quietly as a butterfly's kiss on the face of a flower, Emily breathed her final earthly breath. Her suffering was over. She had fought the good fight, finished the race, and kept the faith (2 Timothy 4:7). She was pronounced dead at 1:55 p.m. At the same moment, God pronounced her free. Koressa would tell me later that she felt the presence of the Virgin Mary in Emily's hospital room. If I could not accompany Emily into eternity, then I can think of no other mother that I would have wanted to go in my place.

The moments following Emily's death are precious to me. We were asked to leave her room briefly, and when we returned, the IVs and supplemental oxygen supply had been removed. The room was still and quiet. Emily, or more appropriately her earthly shell, was sitting in bed with her hands beside her on top of the covers. She looked as though she were sleeping; peace was on her face. I half expected her to open her eyes, throw back the covers, and say she was ready to go home. But, of course, she was already Home.

In the months after Emily's death, we learned that at least four people had had remarkable "spirit" experiences either the night before or immediately following her passing. These events have convinced us that she passed through her beloved Buffalo Gap on her way to eternity, that she was full of joy and free of cancer, and that all was well with her soul. Their stories are worth repeating.

Betty's Story

Betty Jones, Jerry's cousin, has kept a dream journal for a number of years. On the night of December 19, 1995—the night before Emily died—Betty had a most remarkable dream. This is what she wrote the next day:

> Emily came to me to say "goodbye"—I asked her why she had come to me—she said "just to test things out" and to remind me to take care of JoAnna—she was with Mama and Miss Em—they were flying and Emily was smiling that big ole grin of hers. When I woke I knew she was making her transition—I send love and light.

JoAnna is Betty's adopted daughter, who continues to live at home. Betty's mother's name was Dorothy. She passed away in May 1991 at the age of eighty-one. "Miss Em" was our Emily's paternal great-grandmother, after whom Emily was named. Miss Em died in October 1980, also at the age of eighty-one, four months before the birth of her namesake. Emily did not know Miss Em in her earthly life, but surely she knows her in her eternal life.

Marie's Story

Emily received hundreds of cards and letters while she was sick. A precious lady named Marie Shifflett was one of the dear souls who sent cards and balloons to Emily on a regular basis. Emily always looked forward to them and especially liked it when a new balloon from Marie was delivered to her hospital room.

I thought it was a great idea when she asked me to make Marie a set of paper angels like the ones that always hung above her bed, whether she was at home or in the hospital. Marie was so pleased to get her angels that she hung them from the chandelier in the dining room of her beautiful home, which was located on a farm not far from Buffalo Gap High School. Emily went with me the day we delivered Marie's angels. It was in early spring, and beautiful flowers were in bloom in her yard.

On the afternoon of December 20, Marie had finished her lunch and was standing at her sink washing dishes. She dried them, folded the dish towel, and headed for the dining room table, where she planned to sit to write more notes to friends and shut-ins. As she approached the table, the angels somehow dislodged from the chandelier and fell to the floor at her feet. "What are you trying to tell me?" she asked as she stooped to pick them up and return them to the light fixture. At the same moment, the phone rang. She answered it and learned of Emily's passing.

While writing this book, one of Marie's daughters shared with me that her mom often told this story of the angels tumbling from the chandelier. Donna also shared that Marie had written scripture verses on the bottom of each side of the angels. How I cherish the thought that this beautiful, faith-filled woman claimed these verses for my Emily:

2 Corinthians 4:16 Therefore we do not lose heart. Though outwardly we are wasting away, yet inwardly we are being renewed day by day. [Emily's name is written above this scripture.]

James 5:16 Therefore confess your sins to each other and pray for each other so that you may be healed. The prayer of a righteous person is powerful and effective.

1 Corinthians 15:42–44 So will it be with the resurrection of the dead. The body that is sown is perishable, it is raised imperishable; it is sown in dishonor, it is raised in glory; it is sown in weakness, it is raised in power; it is sown a natural body, it is raised a spiritual body. If there is a natural body, there is also a spiritual body.

John 14:1–3 Do not let your hearts be troubled. You believe in God; believe also in me. My Father's house has many rooms; if that were not so, would I have told you that I am going there to prepare a place for you? And if I go and prepare a place for you, I will come back and take you to be with me that you also may be where I am.

1 Peter 1:3–4 Praise be to the God and Father of our Lord Jesus Christ! In his great mercy he has given us new birth into a living hope through the resurrection of Jesus Christ from the dead, and into an inheritance that can never perish, spoil or fade. This inheritance is kept in heaven for you.

Matthew 11:28 Come to me, all you who are weary and burdened, and I will give you rest.

Hebrews 1:14 Are not all angels ministering spirits sent to serve those who will inherit salvation?

Matthew 5:4 Blessed are those who mourn, for they will be comforted.

Kathy's Story

December 20 was the last day of classes before school students in Augusta County began their winter break. The Buffalo Gap High School Choir, of which Emily was a member, traveled to the middle school for a performance. Upon returning to the high school, many of Emily's friends learned of her passing. Kathy Rowe, BGHS choral director, shared with me later that there was much weeping among her close friends.

Emily was well loved at BGHS. Mrs. Rowe was particularly fond of her. She wrote this about her and about the day she died:

One of the greatest blessings of my teaching career was to have the privilege to teach Emily. She was in my Choral Music Class, and each class period that Emily entered my room, it was as if the room radiated with sunshine, not only to me, but to her fellow students who loved her deeply! Emily's beauty came from her inner strength in her valiant battle with the dread disease, Cancer! I never got to see Emily with flowing hair, but only with decorative head turbans which brightened her aura, representing the determination to overcome!

On that cold December day, our Buffalo Gap High School Choral Department visited several neighboring schools as we did prior to each Christmas holiday to recruit younger students for our high school music program. Our two busloads of students returned to Buffalo Gap to find that our Emily had gone to be with Jesus! The grief was overwhelming as we returned into the classroom, so I took Emily's classmates to the Guidance Office for counsel.

As we entered the office, we looked out the window and there falling out of a clear blue sky into the parking lot were beautiful, glistening ice crystals! As we watched these crystals fall, without a cloud in the sky, we knew these works of God were Emily receiving her new body, and that she was now a healthy "re-creation" of Almighty God! What peace we felt as we grieved outwardly but knew she no longer suffered with this dread disease, but now had inherited her new body and had "Peace that passes all understanding"! Every time any who knew Emily see beautiful ice crystals, or hear the song "Angels among Us," we are reminded of that beautiful, brave soul, who taught us how to live life each day with the "light of love."

Ron's Story

Ron Shipp, husband of Susan, Emily's Home I.V. nurse, never met Emily, but he came to love her through Susan and through their two sons, both of whom had been Emily's classmates from late elementary school on. He sent the following account of his experience on the day Emily passed.

I started out the morning of December 20, 1995 to take a drive up in the mountains, to see the beautiful snow and ice. Seeing the white crested mountains from a distance, I decided to try for the top of Reddish Knob, which is the highest mountain top anywhere around, second highest in all Virginia, about 4300 feet high.

As I drove down the Shenandoah Mountain Road near Deerfield into the National Park onto the dirt road, each mile became more and more beautiful. Finally about 15 miles into the forest, I came to the road that goes up the mountain—7 miles to the top. The road was getting slick as it had begun to snow, adding more to the several inches that had fallen the night before. The higher I went the more beautiful it became. The ice on the trees became crystallized and finally at the top where there used to be an old fire tower, you can see 360 degrees all around from West Virginia to Massanutten all the way to Afton Mountain and beyond. The trees' limbs were solid white, as beautiful as I've ever seen.

I arrived about 12 noon, had lunch and spent about one and one-half hours in prayer and meditation. Then I read aloud the poem about Emily and started down. The roads were very, very icy by then and I slid sideways about 100 feet into a bank, then eased ever so slowly ahead coming back down the other side of the mountain. I stopped to see this 50 foot high tree, like a Christmas tree in shape, a beautiful fir tree. It was completely covered in snow, each set of limbs up the tree were more and more white and at the top, a pointed shape almost like an angel of crystallized ice and snow. It was so, so pure white, so, so beautiful, I just cried for joy.

I looked at the clock. It was a little past 2:00 P.M. I thought that's the way Emily is going to be. I looked all around everywhere it was so wonderful, so beautiful. Then a thought came to me. All the branches on the big tree were pointing down, because of the snow on them pointing to the valley below. So I carefully started down. It took a while and I stopped many times as thoughts came to me, rushing through my mind, I can't remember so many beautiful things all at once. The sunlight was shimmering on the icy trees. The mountains were capped in white. There was a glistening glow all around and icicles majestically hung from the rocks. There was also this lake with ice around its edges and water sparkling like the stars and as the snow blew, it swirled, dancing up into the sky. But as I came to the valley below, the temperature was warmer, and everything started to look as it usually does. The trees were green, everything was very nice, but not like on the mountaintop. And I thought, O No! Please don't stop, it's so, so beautiful.

Then I felt like I was supposed to stop the car. So I did and then a message was given to me.

"What you just saw on the mountain top is the way everything really looks, the way everything and everyone really are. The way it looks to Emily. Look closely and you will see the beauty. For what you saw on the mountain top is in the valley, too. Look with the LOVE in your Heart and you will see."

All the way home I was in tears, full of Thanksgiving and felt such peace, such harmony, such unity.

When I arrived home about 4:30 P.M., I called Susan at work. She said, "I have something to tell you." I said, "I already know." She said, "About 2 P.M." I said, "There's something very, very special to tell you."

Thank God for Emily, Thank God for Love.

Emily's Love

To All my Family, and Friends who call me Emily
Your LOVE has been so Wonderful from the start
Thank You, for being there for me
I LOVE You, with All my Heart

LOVE is the Reason that I came here
It's to LOVE, that I now go
LOVE is All I ever hoped to find here
And LOVE, I have Truly come to know

In So many ways I've seen LOVE here
In ways I don't even know
LOVE is Always So Very Near
Day by Day, Our LOVE Continues to Grow

And LOVE is the Reason that I came here
It's to LOVE, that I now go
LOVE is All I ever hoped to find here
LOVE, I have Truly come to know

Our Face of LOVE, with you I leave
And on that Face, there is No woe
From Your Heart to Mine, Love I Do Receive
From My Heart to Yours, LOVE Continues to Flow

To LOVE, Is the Reason that I Come Here
LOVE, I have come to Show
LOVE, Is Always So Very Near
And it's To LOVE, that I now go.

—Ron Shipp

Chapter 16

Wishing you all the best
at this season of the year.

—from a Christmas card that Emily made,

fall 1994

Visitation for Emily was held on Friday, December 22, at a local funeral home. Hundreds of people came, and the visitation lasted well beyond the hour and a half that had been planned. It seems surreal to me even now. As Emily would have wanted, I never shed a tear while I shook hands and hugged friends and family. "Mom, if you're going to cry, leave the room!" This was her celebration, her victory, her moment of rejoicing.

For the Lamb at the center before the throne

will be their shepherd;

he will lead them to springs of living water.

And God will wipe away every tear from their eyes.

—Revelation 7:17

She looked so beautiful resting in her satin bed, Tuppie by her side. The outfit we chose for her was the same one that she'd selected for her formal pictures with Ann and Sebastian—pink blouse with white satin Peter Pan collar and blue-jeans skirt. Shannon, Emily's first cousin, tucked a wallet-sized picture of herself inside the skirt pocket so that she and Emily would not be separated.

An unmistakable peace had settled over Emily's entire being. It wasn't imagined—more than one person commented on it. One friend told me that she had recently experienced overwhelming stress in her family and as a result had questioned her relationship with God. Seeing the radiant peace on Emily's face lifted her own burden, and she left the funeral home with a renewed spirit. In what should have been our darkest, most grief-stricken hour, we were instead filled with celebration and hope and a peace that passes all understanding.

It was the same peace that Jerry had recalled one restless night at the Ronald McDonald House during the first weeks of Emily's illness. It was the peace promised to believers in Philippians 4:7: "And the peace of God, which transcends all understanding, will guard your hearts and your minds in Christ Jesus."

The morning of December 23 dawned bitterly cold and clear. At around ten thirty, the funeral home director, who happened to be our friend and a member of our church, arrived to drive us to the service. Just before we were to leave, however, he accidentally damaged the car door by catching it on the basketball goalpost beside our driveway. He had to exchange vehicles, and it really did look like we might be late for Emily's funeral.

Fortunately, he returned within minutes, and at eleven o'clock, we entered Central United Methodist Church. As we walked down the aisle, more than six hundred friends and family—among them Dave Matthews and many of the hospital teachers and staff—stood in honor of us and in memory of the brave, beautiful adolescent whose casket, covered in a spray of pink flowers, rested before us.

Sunlight burst through the stained-glass windows, bathing the top of Emily's casket with beams of colored light. One of her classmates told me later that he saw Emily dancing above her casket. We sang Emily's favorite hymn, "Lord of the Dance." The sound of six hundred voices reverberated together through the sanctuary: "Dance, then, wherever you may be; I am the Lord of the Dance, said he. And I'll lead you all wherever you may be, And I'll lead you all in the dance, said he." (*The United Methodist Hymnal*, The United Methodist Publishing House, 1989, Ninth Printing, 1993, p. 261.)

Pastor Hugh delivered a poignant and powerful message. In part he said,

Emily's life was short by our usual measure of years . . . but it was a life lived fully and faithfully. She found in the scriptures:

God: to whom she grew closer with each passing day;

Jesus Christ: her Savior and Lord;

The Holy Spirit: her companion and comforter—God's personal messenger to her on a daily basis;

A Faith History: she was able to feel connected to those who had lived before her and to take in many of the mysteries of life;

A Light: so that she did not feel lost in darkness, anxiety, or despair;

A Comfort: so that she could have uncommon patience to endure uncommon suffering and to face death without fear;

Companionship: God's very presence in her journey;

Truth: a sense of what things were all about and an ability to take change in stride;

Strength: to endure so many challenges.

Most of all, Emily found in her faith the **Power of Love:** her family's love for her; the love of her friends; God's love; and the love of strangers and people who went out of their way to share life with her. . . .

Cancer, rather than closing Emily down, *expanded* her life and her field of relationships. She had so much impact on so many . . . *not the least* of whom were those of us right here at home who knew her. She came to church as often as she could. As long as she was able, she continued to be a Young Proclaimer at worship services. She participated in youth activities, and attended worship services. Just two weeks ago, before she entered UVA Hospital again, though it took a wheelchair and all the energy she had, Emily was at worship. . . .

Christmas was very special to Emily. When she was little, she drew a picture of a trumpet, and wrote on it, "I will be a trumpeter for God." Somehow I can picture her this Christmas with a host of angels, *trumpet in hand,* glorifying God in ways we can only dream about. . . .

Truly, Emily's life is something to *celebrate* today, and so we do. Yes, the grief is deep and real. Yes, we miss her, and always will. Yes, it's painful and hard. *But death is not the last word here . . . Life is the last word!* Emily has gone forth *to live,* in her *spirit, eternally* in God's blessing. She has come *full circle* in giving glory to God.

Near the conclusion of Emily's service, many listeners dabbed their eyes as the recording David Kleiner and the other musicians had made of Emily's "Cancer for Christmas" was played. Many of her favorite scriptures were also read. Emily's spirit was present in Central United Methodist Church that Saturday morning, and it was good.

Emily was laid to rest in Thornrose Cemetery, located less than a mile west of our church and directly behind our house. In fact, Emily's bedroom window was clearly visible from her gravesite. We were fortunate to get four plots in this location, made available only after an ancient tree had fallen some months earlier. Emily had had no interest in knowing what would happen to her in the event she did not survive her cancer and never discussed any of her wishes other than those expressed in her little will. Nonetheless, I think she would have approved our selection.

As a young child, Emily seemed to know that she would always be connected to the Alleghany house. In fact, she even told her daddy that she would never leave home. Jerry responded exactly as any parent would have; he told her that of course she would leave home—that's what children did when they grew up. But Emily remained insistent that she would never leave. She was right. Someday Jerry and I will join her in that peaceful place near the house that she loved so much.

Jerry and I asked eight dear friends to be active pallbearers. Each one had played a significant role during Emily's illness: Andy Sayers, Ann's high school sweetheart, had made life seem fun and normal when it was anything but; David Leatherwood, church friend and prayer warrior, had come to the house as soon as he heard of Emily's passing, organized food, and took care of our every need in the first lonely hours; Gary Persinger, a middle-school teacher, had prayed with and encouraged Emily into her final hours; Randy Lindamood, another church friend, had put poinsettias and lilies in church at Christmas and Easter in Emily's name and continued to do so for many years; George Savage, another middle-school teacher, had given Emily hand-carved walking sticks and was a wonderful prayer warrior and top-notch science teacher; Al Costa, the principal of my school, had been gracious beyond words in accommodating my extended absences and sporadic teaching schedule while Emily was ill; Steve Huffer, a church prayer warrior, had been sensitive to God's calling to minister to Emily with words of encouragement and to be present with her the day she died; and

David Motes, our very dear friend, who had loved Emily as though she were his own.

Extreme cold kept friends and family from lingering at the cemetery. One person stayed, however, waiting to grieve with me. Dave Matthews, who just thirteen days before had sung sweet songs to Emily, put his arms around me and wept. This kind and gentle man will have a special place in my heart forever.

Many people came to our house from the cemetery. The rooms were filled with warm chatter and plenty of laughter, as friends and family recalled loving memories and happy tales of Emily's antics. By nightfall, everyone but Ann, Bubbles, Jerry, and I had gone. The Christmas tree was lit, and packages, including those selected by Emily just a few days earlier, were underneath the low branches. Stockings with Ann's and Emily's names were hung below the mantle. The Christmas garland cheered up the front-yard fence, each swag a little lighted smile. And so it was that the reality of life without Emily began to settle in. Instead of a family of five, we were now a family of four.

In eighth grade, Emily had taken Latin I. Before the winter break, her class had a project in which students were to design a holiday card. Emily had made hers specifically for Jerry, who had studied Latin in high school and college. She had decorated the outside with holly leaves and red berries and printed a Latin phrase on the inside. Translated, it said, "Wishing you all the best at this season of the year."

Jerry had been very proud of his card and displayed it on the desk in the living room throughout the 1994 holiday season. When it was time to store it, the card had disappeared. We looked everywhere, but it was gone. A year passed. Then, early on December 24, while Ann, Bubbles, and I slept, Jerry walked into the living room and happened to notice the corner of a piece of paper jutting out from under the desk. He reached down and pulled it out. After a year of vacuuming and dusting and moving chairs in that location, Emily's Latin holiday card had suddenly appeared. *Wishing you all the best at this season of the year.*

Jerry came into our bedroom, tears pouring from his eyes, incredulous, saying, "Is this a coincidence?" We both knew the answer. That night we attended the Christmas Eve service at Central United Methodist Church, knowing that a true Christmas miracle had arrived early that morning.

Christmas Day was bittersweet and much too quiet. We slept in, actually. Emily would not have allowed such a thing. After breakfast, the four of us gathered in the living room to open packages. Emily's hand-picked gifts brought tears to our eyes, especially when Bubbles opened hers—a stained-glass heart with a series of smaller hearts on the inside and the words, "I Love You with All My Hearts." Emily gave Jerry a children's book she knew he loved—*If You Give a Mouse a Cookie,* by Laura Joffe Numeroff. Inside the book she had pasted a picture of herself smiling, standing beside a very large costumed mouse at a local bookstore. She also wrote,

> Merry Christmas!
> Dear Dad,
> You are the best dad a girl could have. I don't know what I would do without you. You are always buying me things, such as clothes and decorations for the porch, but what I like to get most of all is the love you poor [sic] out to Ann and I. You are such a loving dad. I loved that day it was just you and me. What more could a daughter want? I love you daddy and know that you love me more than anything too! I am so glad God gave me you. I love you always! You are the #1 dad and always will be. I love you and hope you like your gift. Merry Christmas Dad!!
> Love you always, Emily
> Christmas 1995

Jerry cried as he read what Emily had written. He said that it was the best Christmas gift he had ever received. To this day, he keeps the book locked away as one of his most cherished possessions.

Eighteen Christmases have now come and gone since Emily left us. Not one day has passed that I haven't thought of her. It is comforting to know she is nestled in the hearts of others as well. At least four girls have been named after her.

Jessica Henson, whose smile could light up a room, was a classmate and dear friend to Emily. She and her sweet grandmother visited Emily in the hospital many times. I can still hear the girly giggles as the two teens joked and laughed about middle-school "things." Jessica's Emily is beautiful, intelligent, and always smiling, just like her mother.

I was surprised and greatly delighted the day I learned that yet another classmate had named her firstborn daughter after Emily. Debbie told me how much she had loved and admired Emily Jones and that she was so happy to name her daughter after her courageous friend. Words can scarcely describe the honor of this tribute.

Shannon, Jerry's niece, named her firstborn after her beloved cousin. Alayna Emily is now a beautiful "tween." It is my hope that this book will better acquaint her with her cousin Emily.

Then there is my first granddaughter, Emily Caroline Long, whose curiosity about and love for her Auntie Emily fills my heart with unspeakable joy and gratitude. In fact, I often see traces—little ice crystals—of Auntie Emily in both of my granddaughters. My life sparkles as a result.

I do not know if Emily Caroline Jones would have married or if she would have had children. But of these things I am positive: She has a legacy not only in four darling girls but in the countless people whose lives she touched—*and* I will see her again.

Dr. De Alarcon was right: we did get our miracle—not the physical healing for which we yearned, but a spiritual healing that was pure and perfect. Emily walked through the fiery furnace and came out as refined gold. She was courageous, sensitive, spunky, and full of love. She never blamed God for her cancer. Instead, she relied on Him for strength. His word sustained her and gave her courage in the face of a horrifying disease. And, yes, she was a teacher—she taught us how to live and how to die.

She was witness to a steadfast confidence in an eternal future and the assurance that death of the physical body is not the end. As Jesus told his apostles, "Do not let your hearts be troubled. Trust in God; trust also in me. In my Father's house are many rooms; if it were not so, I would have told you. I am going there to prepare a place for you" (John 14:1–2). Above all, she taught us—to paraphrase Corrie Ten Boom—there is no pit so deep that Jesus the Christ has not gone nor will not go deeper.

Emily Caroline Jones walked by faith. She maintained her faith walk until her final breath.

1995

God revealed his goodness to us in distinct ways following Emily's death. He showed us specifically how He "worked behind the scenes" to provide comfort and assurance that Emily's life was not in vain. Indeed, our God is an awesome God and worthy is His name to be praised.

Gift from a Perpetual Scripture Calendar

During the last three months of Emily's life, she slept on the family room futon, and I slept in the recliner nearby. I loved the nights when we talked until one or the other of us dozed off. Now that she was gone, there was no reason to sleep downstairs. The time had come to sleep in my own bed next to my husband, just as I had before Emily got sick.

However, before climbing the stairs to our bedroom that first night after her death, I sat in the recliner and looked at the empty futon. In my mind's eye, I saw her back, her deep auburn curls jumbled across her head. I heard her call, "Good night, Bubbles," just as she had done countless nights before. I watched her slender, china-white fingers scratch a favorite spot behind Sebastian's ear. Then she turned and looked at me, smiling, "I love you, Mom." Oh, to have her blow me a kiss that I could seal in my heart. I have never missed anyone so much in my life. It was almost unbearable.

> And my God will meet all your needs according to his glorious riches in Christ Jesus.
>
> —*Philippians 4:19*

A short while later, I slipped my exhausted body between the sheets on our bed. It was quiet upstairs, and I allowed my thoughts to whirl in my head. As I would many times over the coming months, I thought of Emily's final ride across Afton Mountain, alone in a box in the back of a hearse. The thought was haunting and made me shiver. I could not stand the idea of her being alone and in the dark. I still can't. "No, Caroline," I protested with myself, "her *body* came home in a box—Emily was not there."

Just then, Jerry appeared in the doorway, tears streaming down his cheeks. He held a perpetual scripture calendar, a gift to us years earlier from Betsy Curry, my friend who saw thousands of prayers flying heavenward on Emily's behalf. "Read this," he sobbed, as he handed me the calendar, turned to the entry for December 20:

A teardrop on earth summons

the King of Heaven.

—Charles R. Swindoll

(Growing Strong in the

Seasons of Life, p. 163)

It was a paraphrase from Job 16:19–21, which reads: "Even now my witness is in heaven; my advocate is on high. My intercessor is my friend as my eyes pour out tears to God; on behalf of a man he pleads with God as a man pleads for his friend."

"Oh, Father," I thought, "what have you done? Did not teardrops fall from Emily's eyes this very afternoon, her final act as a living child of God? And now you, the Creator, the Author of Life, the Alpha and Omega, have given us a perfect gift, a promise that the King of Heaven was summoned on behalf of our dying child." Coincidence? No! Miracle? Yes!—a gift from a Father who knew our needs and provided for them before we knew them ourselves. It was perfect assurance that Emily was with the Creator; that she was in His presence, safe and at peace. Hot, healthy, cleansing tears flooded my eyes. Praise God from whom all blessings flow!

The Angel Pin

We know that angels surrounded Emily throughout the final week of her life. All of us sensed their presence on multiple occasions. I would soon learn how angels had "touched" another friend immediately after Emily's death.

Doris was not so much "into" angels; yet when she heard that Emily had passed, she was overwhelmed with thoughts of these heavenly beings—an exceptionally odd feeling for her. Wanting to do something for our family and stay within her tight budget, she happened to pick up a sale flyer for a local store. There, on the front page, was an ad for an angel pin at $9.99—the perfect price. She knew instantly that she was meant to get this little pin—a miniature angel holding a heart in her hand. She had no idea why, just that she had to get it.

Within minutes, she was in her car headed for the store. She arrived at the jewelry counter and asked for a pin like the one in the flyer. "We're sold out of them," she was told. Doris was devastated; she *knew* she was to purchase the pin. Then, she told me, "I walked away and was immediately directed by that still, quiet voice inside of me to go back and talk to the salesperson."

Determined Doris turned around at the door and went back to the saleslady. With her deep brown eyes focused on the clerk, Doris told the story of Emily's death and how she *knew* that Emily's mother simply had to have this angel pin. Then Doris said, "I bet if you looked around, you would find one."

The bewildered saleslady began searching through some items that had been put under the counter. There, nestled in a place where it did not belong, was a tiny gold angel, a heart in her hand. The saleslady said that she could not believe that one little pin had gotten tucked away under the counter. "Believe, madam. Believe." But there it was, and she sold it to Doris, who brought it to the funeral home with the message that the Lord had directed her to deliver it to me.

The angel's message was instantly revealed to me: Emily's heart was with the Lord. Psalm 91:11 says, "For he will command his angels concerning you to guard you in all your ways." An angelic ministry begun on earth now extended into eternity. Warm joy flooded over me and I was at peace.

Joyce's Card

A little more than a week after Emily's death, we received a sympathy card from a friend and colleague. Joyce, also a guidance counselor, had worked with Jerry for years. She wrote in her card, "I hope the enclosed letter will fulfill Isaiah 51:12 for you ('I, even I am He who comforts you.')." In part, the prophecy given to us in Joyce's letter became the seed for this book.

> December 26, 1995
> Dearest Friends in Christ,
> As I ponder the work of the Holy Spirit over the last two years, I am humbled and in awe of His love for us.
> I recall how He awoke me in the middle of the night early on in Emily's illness and how He had prepared my spirit to pray for her very life thru a book I was reading about Jesus' ministry here on earth. Secondly, in conversation over the phone late last spring, I was commiserating with someone about how unfortunate her [Emily's] declining condition was and before the day was thru, did so with two other people at school. The Lord reminded me that like Peter, I had denied His hand in Emily's life 3 times. He said, "You don't know what I've done and continue to do in the lives of those touched by Emily."
> It seems there is a third way in which He wishes to reveal His love to you, this time through a word of prophecy. Please believe it is of Him, because I had many directions I could have gone in offering human encouragement but I've *learned* that if it's to really minister to a need, I *must wait* on the Spirit.
> The Lord would say to you: "*Be assured that Emily's life*

was not in vain. You have found strength and peace in the midst of pain because you have not denied My sovereignty over Emily's and your lives. *Your faithfulness to Me will be a witness to many* and like the unending waves of the ocean, I will continue to pour out my blessings on you."

'All is well.'

In His love,

Joyce Wampler

Sebastian's Story

On the day Emily died, Koressa Malcolm took Sebastian to Highland County so that he would not be underfoot or stressed by all the company who would be in our house. She brought him back a week later. As I often did in the cold of winter, I walked him in the yard rather than on long jaunts around the neighborhood. On our first walk, he trotted directly up the hill toward the cemetery fence. Specifically, he headed for the lower right side of the fence—the area closest to Emily's grave. What happened next astounded me.

He stood on his hind legs and looked directly at her gravesite. He remained "standing" for perhaps twenty-five or thirty seconds, then went down on all fours and trotted off to another part of the yard. Each day that week, he did the same thing—pulled me toward the back fence, stood on his hind legs, and looked in the direction of her grave.

A blizzard hit our area a week after Sebastian came home. Deep snow prevented him from getting into the backyard. After the snow melted, he had no interest in returning to the lower-right portion of the cemetery fence.

About two weeks later, Jerry had a dream that Emily was walking a dog in the cemetery. It was a big dog, and Emily was very happy. The picture of Emily, content and at peace, brought the same contentment and peace to Jerry. He knew all was well with her.

Ten years later, Sebastian's health failed, and he had to be put down. He was cremated and his ashes were spread on Emily's grave, the only place where he would have wanted to be.

Call to Prayer

Much happened in our family during the year following Emily's death. Ann graduated from Buffalo Gap High School and entered the College of William and Mary the following fall. On February 11, 1996, Bubbles suffered a devastating stroke and was paralyzed on her left side. Her cognition and reasoning were also impaired. She had to move to a local nursing home. Only Jerry and I and Emily's two pets—Sebastian and Fish—were living at home.

One Saturday early in December 1996, I traveled to Charlottesville to Christmas shop. I was on my way home when I suddenly felt an overwhelming urge to pray. I had no idea why or for whom, so I opened my mouth and prayed whatever words came forth.

As I approached my exit from the interstate, I realized that traffic was at a standstill in the northbound lanes. It was obvious that there had been an accident, and I decided that the Lord wanted me to pray for someone who might be injured or even dead. I said another prayer for this unknown person, then eased my car onto the exit ramp, which was open for cars going into Staunton. As I drove toward home, I again felt compelled, this time not to pray but to go to the cemetery.

The late fall sun was low in the sky when I pulled to a stop near Emily's grave. Her gray granite headstone had been in place nearly six months. Joy, a friend and amateur artist, had designed an angel blowing a trumpet, her dainty feet like those of a dancer visible from the bottom of her long, flowing robe. Joy's exact drawing was carved on Emily's stone. A banner above the angel says, "I will be a trumpeter for God." When, as a first or second grader, Emily had penned those words beneath a slightly misshapen drawing of a trumpet, she wrote "trumpter." We decided not to use her spelling to keep the engraver from being blamed for an error he did not make.

In the chill of that afternoon, I placed my hand on Emily's stone. Words began to spill from my mouth: "If only I could put my hands in your red curly hair just one more time," I pleaded. "If only I could put my arms around you and dance just one more time. . . ." Then, as quickly as frosty winter breath vanishes, the words ceased to come. I got in the car and drove home.

Without warning, at 9:13 that night, I *had* to call Ann, who had not yet come home from college for her holiday break. I clearly remember looking at the clock and hoping it wasn't too late to call. Without a clue as to why I had to talk to Ann, I picked up the phone and dialed her dorm room. The phone rang and she answered. We chatted briefly, then she said in a rather serious tone, "Mom, are you sitting down? There's something I need to tell you." My heart and stomach sank right to the gutter. I was sure I was going to hear words that every parent dreads.

"Yes, I'm sitting down."

"Last night I had a dream," she began. "I dreamt that I put my hands in Emily's red curly hair just one more time; I dreamt that I put my arms around her, and we danced just one more time."

It was all I could do not to drop the receiver. I was speechless, completely and totally speechless. Ann had repeated nearly word for word what I uttered in the cemetery. I told her that I would call her back the next night. I was simply too stunned to say more at that moment.

The next night, I did call Ann to explain my reaction. She wept and I wept, not over yet another coincidence but over the knowledge that the God whom we worship is awesome beyond comprehension. What am I except a grain of sand in the great scheme of things? I am nothing and I am everything. Once again, my God was there before me, reassuring me that He is in control and all is well.

Just as my prayer-warrior friend Karen used to say, God is never late, and He doesn't make mistakes. He will not abandon His children, and He goes to great lengths to reveal that promise to those who will receive it.

I share a belief with a former pastor that God brought heaven and Earth close together in the person of Jesus the Christ. That thought keeps Emily close to me. I also know that she knew who she was and whose she was. She put on the armor of God and faced unspeakable pain and suffering with incredible courage and conviction. She loved life and desired it passionately. I take comfort in knowing that because of a man named Jesus, *eternal life* is hers. All is well, indeed.

Amen and Amen.

"It Happened to Me"—
One Girl Copes with Cancer[1]

By Emily Caroline Jones

Girls' Life, October/November 1994,

Volume 1, Issue 2:20–21

"I'm sorry to have to tell you this but, Emily, you have cancer." These are the words that changed my life. It all began last Thanksgiving weekend when I was 12. I got very sick and could not keep anything in my stomach. I was having an awful pain like nothing I had ever felt. Finally, my pain went away but the episode went on about once a week for the next month or so.

When we got out of school for Christmas vacation, everything got worse. I went to the doctor, who did a bunch of tests. My doctor could not figure it out. I was fine during the day but sick at night. My doctor gave me some gas relief stuff and a medicine for acid in my stomach. It didn't work.

One day, I threw up in his clinic and had some awful pain, so he saw for himself what I was going through. He put me in a hospital in Staunton, VA., where doctors put a tube down my nose to my stomach. After a lot of tests and X-rays, they found a blockage in my intestine. I needed surgery to remove it. Doctors there did not want to do the surgery because I was so young. So I was sent to the University of Virginia Children's Medical Center.

---

[1]Reprinted by permission of *Girls' Life* magazine.

When I got there, the doctors asked a lot of questions. Then on Friday, Jan. 14, I went in for surgery. The doctors removed my blockage and looked around in my abdomen. I had a sinking feeling when my doctor told me I have cancer. He said there were a lot of seed tumors and a few big tumors.

At first, the doctors thought I had intestinal cancer. On Friday, Jan. 21, I had a second surgery to remove my ovaries, which were very cancerous. Then they made slides of my ovaries, changed their decision and said I had ovarian cancer. The doctors sent my slides to the best ovarian cancer doctor in America, who said it was not have [sic] ovarian cancer.

After a lot of tests and indecisiveness about what form of cancer I have, it was final—I have adenocarcinoma of the small bowel. This is an intestinal cancer that usually comes in old people. Of course, I don't fit that category.

My cancer is very rare, even in adults. My doctors think I might be the youngest case ever reported. Well, this was exciting news in a way because I would be in magazines, but the excitement stopped when I started my chemotherapy. I had migraine headaches, which stopped after I had some medicine. The next problem was painful ulcers in my mouth. One of the nurses said it looked like a lawn mower had gone through my mouth.

Well, on with the story. I get chemo every month. I come into the clinic one week every month. Every day of that week I get chemo. Three days every week I get a shot. The week right before my chemo week I have nothing.

This is how my life has been for nearly a year. Soon, I will go through some more tests. I have been taking tests every two months. Once I am pretty much back to normal, I will have some exploratory surgery to make sure everything is gone. I do not know what will happen next. I guess if they find more cancer they will continue with chemo, but who knows.

There is one other story I would like to tell. When my school's seventh-grade chorus went to another school, I told my friend I needed a book because I had not memorized the songs. Well, a girl from another school said, "Why not?"

I said, "I've been in the hospital. I have cancer." Then she said, "Does that mean you are going to die?" That really shocked me. I would like to tell people that even though we have no hair and a life-threatening disease does not necessarily mean we're going to die, and you should not be scared of us.

I lost my hair from the chemo treatment, but I have some hair that I call "Cindy" because I don't like the word "wig." I don't always wear Cindy; I also have a lot of fun hats to wear. And I like to eat pizza and chili dogs, even though some days I can't eat them because of the stomach upset. I am a normal, everyday person trying to lead my life and make the best of a bad situation.

Thank you for listening. I hope you liked reading my story.

(NOTE: Emily's Valentine's poem, which was part of this article, may be found on pages 75–76.)

"Cancer for Christmas"

By Emily Caroline Jones
with the guidance and musical
talents of David Kleiner
Spring 1995

It all began on a December day.
Would it be over by May?
Christmas was coming, I was very sick.
I was filled with joy.
Would my healing come quick?

When Christmas comes and kids get candy and toys,
Learning I had cancer didn't bring me much joy.
I was sick, and I was sad.
Santa, I wasn't bad.
Why couldn't you bring me something else?
Why couldn't you bring me something else?

Went to the doctor to see what was wrong—
Didn't know the journey would be so long—
Went to the medical center,
Ended up with cancer—
Would my life ever be the same?
Will I ever be a dancer?

When Christmas comes and kids get candy and toys,
Learning I had cancer didn't bring me much joy.

I was sick, and I was sad.
Santa, I wasn't bad.
Why couldn't you bring me something else?
Why couldn't you bring me something else?

You think you can't get this illness.
Everybody has a chance of getting this sickness.
Only kid in the world with this disease—
Am I going to be teased?
Every day I fight a battle.
Every day opens a new door.
Every day I tell myself, one day I'll win this war.

When Christmas comes and kids get candy and toys,
Learning I had cancer didn't bring me much joy.
I was sick, and I was sad.
Santa, I wasn't bad.
Why couldn't you bring me something else?
Why couldn't you bring me something else?

"My Angel (Emily)"

By Abigail Boone Spann,
oldest sister of Kadee Boone, Emily's friend
March 19, 1996

I knew an angel, but for just a short time
I couldn't see what she was until now
She went through so much; her sufferings were great
But there was a smile on her face anyhow

My angel was amazing, so loving and sweet
Nothing could scare her, not even death
She knew a peace like no one else could
And it stayed with her to the very last breath

Her faith was incredible, she never gave up
This angel knew she could do it all
So she just kept pushing and fighting
Knowing God would never let her fall

My angel knew her time was coming soon
As she began to grow weaker each day
So she made sure to say her last good byes
Before He came to take her away

Yes, my angel is gone, but yet she's still here
For I can still feel her near me
And one day, we'll be together again
When I'm in heaven, with my sweet angel Emily

—For my sweet angel, Emily Jones, and Family

"Pandora's Box"

Words and music by David Kleiner

Sent to Emily's family in March 1999

In David's words:

Here are the lyrics of the song I wrote about my experience working with Emily. Although some details in the song are imagined, I took my cue from Emily and tried to make an honest song. I based the song on the myth of Pandora, which, I remembered while doing some research, is a sequel to the story of Prometheus, who stole fire from the gods to give it to man. As a result, he was condemned to be chained to a mountain and to have his liver torn out every day. As a further punishment, the gods created the most beautiful woman and sent her to earth with her now infamous box. And you know the rest of the story.

I concluded, in getting ready to write the song, that Emily was as much Prometheus (bringing fire with her charisma and the honesty of her song as well as suffering like Prometheus)— as she was Pandora (always full of hope), and that was the origin of the lyrics.

"For Emily, who was part Pandora and part Prometheus"

Verse 1

The last time I saw Cathy
she looked like she was floating,
searching through her treasure box
and listening to her song.
She never really smiled
or said goodbye to me,
though later she said everything
was the way it was meant to be.

Lessons from Emily

Chorus

When you steal fire from heaven
you might touch the flame.
But when we suffer like we suffer,
there is no one you can blame.
The gods might bring us misery,
still we muddle through.
I'd find something to believe
if I could be like you.

Verse 2

Who told you to deal in truths
no one wants to hear?
A child is still and all a child
even when she sees things clear.
You were not bad, did not deserve
what all of us embrace.
You just had more than your share
of bad luck, courage, hope and grace.

Chorus

When you steal fire from heaven
you might touch the flame.
But when we suffer like we suffer,
there is no one you can blame.
The gods might bring us misery,
still we muddle through.

I'd find something to believe
if I could be like you.

Verse 3

What makes people think that cancer
makes a hero out of you?
We all die when we find
there's nothing else that we can do.
Sometimes I get tired
and lay me down to sleep.
You left me a melody
and promises too hard to keep.

Chorus

When you steal fire from heaven
you might touch the flame.
But when we suffer like we suffer,
there is no one you can blame.
The gods might bring us misery,
still we muddle through.
I'd find something to believe
if I could be like you.

Verse 4

When I got to the churchyard
it must have been too late.
The mourners had all gone
and left their offerings at the gate:

ribbons colored lavender,
a pair of dancer's shoes,
a picture of Pandora,
and a photograph of you.

Chorus
When you steal fire from heaven
you might touch the flame.
But when we suffer like we suffer,
there is no one you can blame.
The gods might bring us misery,
still we muddle through.
I'd find something to believe
if I could be like you.

"Unnatural Alloys"

By Lynn Woodson,
editor of the University of Virginia
Hospital's CMC Pinwheel publication
November 12, 1996

Special. That was how she saw it first.

"A rare, unusual cancer," the doctors said, "especially in one so young."

Exotic, thinks Emily, and she names her wig, like a stuffed bear or a family pet.

And she tells her special story, without her older sister. She collects hats with 12-year-old gusto.

She blossoms in hospital art, writing poems, designing a quilt.

Illness can make you stronger, her parents think, watching the body sink into itself, less flesh every day.

Finally, the face almost unrecognizable.

Yellow with drugs, clutched to her mother's side, a sunken-eye pincushion for doctor's needles and tubes.

I remember the night we took pictures, limping through hospital corridors, seeing the walls through Emily's eyes.

Less than an hour later, weak from walking, Emily shoots still lifes from bed.

"Only things that are alive," she directs, pointing to a flower, a pumpkin, a piece of fruit.

I remember Emily best when she read her poem aloud.

*Steady on stage, her morphine pac hanging off her
    shoulder like a schoolgirl's purse.*

*She makes a joke, strikes a pose, and brings down the
    house.*

*Months later, her room draped in yellow lamplight.
    White starched angels made by an aunt. Tears. But
    no Emily. No.*

"Emily"

By Heather Landes,
a caring friend, daughter of Emily's
elementary school music teacher
February 1996

A young girl loving life,
Even though her pain cut like a knife.
She promised not to give up without a fight,
As she died, this child still fought with all her might.

Through all the tests and all her tears,
She did not once show her fears.
She was strong for those who cared,
Though the sadness they felt she also shared.

Her smile still big, her face still bright,
With strength she waited for that magical light.
Knowing she was near the end,
She waited for angels she knew God would send.

About the Author

Caroline Carter Jones was born and grew up in Charlottesville, Virginia. She earned her BS and MEd from the University of Virginia. She married her classmate Jerry Lynn Jones at the University of Virginia chapel in December 1972. They settled in Staunton, Virginia, where they raised their daughters, Ann and Emily.

Caroline worked as a public school special education teacher until the last six months of Emily's life, when she stayed home to care for Emily full time. She returned to public school teaching after Emily died; however, she was so inspired by the Hospital Education Program (HEP) at the University of Virginia Hospital, where Emily had been a patient, that Caroline accepted a position with that program and worked full and part time in the HEP until her retirement.

She and her husband now live in Waynesboro, Virginia. They have three wonderful grandchildren. Caroline loves to cross-stitch in her spare time, but her dream has always been to tell Emily's story so that others may find the love of God in Emily's lessons.